MainstreamGreen
SustainableDesignByLPA

Mainstream Green

Sustainable Design By LPA

images
Publishing

Published in Australia in 2005 by
The Images Publishing Group Pty Ltd
ABN 89 059 734 431
6 Bastow Place, Mulgrave, Victoria 3170, Australia
Tel: +61 3 9561 5544 Fax: +61 3 9561 4860
books@images.com.au
www.imagespublishing.com

National Library of Australia Cataloguing-in-Publication entry:

LPA (Firm)
Mainstream green: sustainable design.

ISBN 1 86470 122 6

1. LPA (Firm). 2. U.S. Green Building Council. 3. Sustainable architecture.
4. Sustainable buildings. 5. Ecological houses. I. Title.

720.47

Coordinating editor: Robyn Beaver

Designed by The Graphic Image Studio Pty Ltd, Mulgrave, Australia
www.tgis.com.au

Digital production and print by Everbest Printing Co. Ltd. in Hong Kong/China

IMAGES has included on its website a page for special notices in relation to this and our other publications.
Please visit www.imagespublishing.com.

Contents

The green building movement is one born of passion—of the desire to make a radical change in the way we think about and design buildings. Just over a decade ago, before we founded the U.S. Green Building Council (USGBC), a growing awareness of the huge threats posed to our natural world by our built environment made it obvious that radical change was imperative. Less obvious was how to make that change happen—we needed a way to turn our passion into the transformation of an entire industry. We founded USGBC to unite the building industry and lead a national consensus on green building, and 12 years later the transformation is well underway. Firms like LPA have been instrumental in that transformation, helping to make "green" an indispensable part of our lexicon.

A growing body of evidence about the significant—and positive—impact green buildings have on the environment, public infrastructure, and on human health and productivity in our homes, schools, and workplaces is helping to further the transformation of our built environment, changing how cities, companies, and institutions think about and plan building development.

The numbers make it clear that green buildings have entered the mainstream. The current LEED® (Leadership in Energy and Environmental Design) products (LEED for New Construction, LEED for Existing Buildings, and LEED for Commercial Interiors) encompass more than 260 million square feet of our built environment, and the suite of LEED products continues to expand to address every building type and phase of a building's lifecycle. Nearly 6,000 companies have joined USGBC as of mid-2005, and more than 70 regional groups support the USGBC mission in their communities. The green building movement has been featured in mainstream media from the *Wall*

INTRODUCTION
BY S. RICHARD FEDRIZZI—
PRESIDENT, CEO, AND FOUNDING CHAIRMAN OF THE U.S. GREEN BUILDING COUNCIL

Green roof atop the Design Center at Ford Motor Company's Premier Automotive Group in Irvine, California.

Street Journal to the History Channel, and it seems like nearly every week another city or state commits to improving the health of its communities by adopting LEED.

Undoubtedly, USGBC and LEED have been crucial to the growth of the green building movement. But our work would be meaningless without firms like LPA, without designers, planners, architects, and builders who share our deep commitment to sustainability and strive to make it a part of everything they do.

Sustainability informs every aspect of LPA's culture, from its own LEED-CI certified office space to the services it offers clients. At LPA, green isn't extra—it's fundamental—and it doesn't think it should be an extra for its clients, either. LPA believes firmly that sustainable design can and should be delivered at no additional cost. From corporate office campuses to elementary schools, LPA makes green design attainable, affordable, and perhaps most important, desirable.

Above: LPA's proprietary LID software supports the firm's green building designs. **Right:** LPA's Irvine, California headquarters is a "living laboratory" that tests green design theories, technologies, and materials.

LPA has made significant contributions to the green building movement, but these contributions are nearly overshadowed by their contributions to architectural practice. Dozens of honors and awards offer ample proof of LPA's commitment to design excellence, but one has only to look at the graceful lines of the Cesar Chavez Elementary School to understand how artfully LPA blends function and aesthetics. In the long term, this may be as important to the success of the green building movement as the environmental and economic benefits of sustainable design—green buildings must delight our senses as well as our bottom lines.

LPA offers us a shining example of what green buildings can and should be. This example will inspire us all, and help guide the way to a future in which sustainability is fundamental to every organization. As excited as I am to cite the statistics about the growth of green buildings, I'm more excited about the day when there *aren't* any "green building" statistics—because all buildings are green. USGBC is working to effect a true market transformation: a future in which building codes start at LEED Certified levels; in which Wall Street evaluates real estate portfolios for their green market potential; where technologies for green products and materials soar while associated costs tumble; a future in which buildings restore instead of consume.

I wake up every morning thrilled by how far we have come, and I know that one day we will look back on this moment as only the beginning.

The staircase tower at Cesar Chavez Elementary School in Long Beach, California is a dramatic architectural statement bathed in natural light from a rooftop skylight.

Cesar Chavez Elementary School in Long Beach, California shows that a school can be green and get good grades for design and function.

CHAPTER 2

Since the 1990s, the media has often talked about "green" or "sustainable" buildings. But what exactly is a green building?

A building is green if:

- Its construction reduces the consumption of natural resources, like wood from old growth forests.

- Most of its construction waste is recycled or reused rather than sent to landfills.

- Its operation reduces the consumption (and costs) of energy and water.

- The development footprint is limited, open space is restored and enhanced, and landscape architecture is designed to provide wildlife habitat, stormwater management, and beauty with minimal water consumption and maintenance.

- The site and building designs minimize or eliminate heat islands—asphalt and other dark, non-reflective surfaces on roofs, walkways, roads, and parking lots that absorb and slowly release solar heat. Heat islands raise surrounding temperatures by as much as 10 degrees, increasing both heating, ventilation, and air conditioning (HVAC) loads and landscape irrigation needs.

- The majority of the interior spaces have natural daylighting and outdoor views.

- Highly efficient HVAC systems and low VOC (Volatile Organic Compound) materials like paint, flooring, and furniture are used to improve the indoor environmental air quality.

- Building materials, from structural steel to carpeting and furniture, have recycled content.

A GREEN PRIMER

The green Toyota South Campus expansion in Torrance, California abounds in attractive open spaces that are landscaped with drought-tolerant plants and shrubs.

The roofs at Wal-Mart's experimental sustainable Supercenter in McKinney, Texas have photovoltaic panels that generate a portion of the store's electrical requirements. Skylights provide natural light, which reduces energy consumption.

The benefits of going green

We must address the impact of our buildings on the environment. Every year in the US, buildings account for 30 percent of raw materials use and 36 percent of the country's total energy consumption, including 65 percent of its electricity use. Buildings produce 30 percent of the US greenhouse gas emissions that contribute to global warming, and they generate 136 million tons of construction and demolition waste annually. And that's just in the US.

The well documented "sick building syndrome" of the late 1980s woke up the world to the fact that our buildings can also harm our health. Standard materials like paint, carpeting, linoleum, furniture, and manufactured wood products, emit toxic fumes that have been directly linked to health problems like asthma, weakened immune systems, and even cancer. Lack of sufficient natural daylighting has been linked to emotional health problems like depression.

Green buildings, in contrast, provide a healthier quality of life, because they use non-toxic building materials, and they provide abundant fresh air and natural light. That healthier quality of life brings many benefits.

Green schools, for example, demonstrably improve learning. A 1999 study by the Heschong Mahone Group of the Fort Collins, Colorado, Orange County, California, and Seattle, Washington school districts found that students in classrooms with the most daylighting progressed 20 percent faster on math tests and 26 percent faster on reading tests than students in classrooms with the least daylighting.

Any type of building and its users will benefit from natural lighting, which reduces energy consumption, makes people feel better, improves mental processes, and reduces fatigue.

Businesses benefit from green buildings in many ways: greater employee productivity, lower turnover rates, and less absenteeism. Green buildings also save companies money over the long term, because they reduce employee health costs (and insurance premiums) and significantly lower energy usage, water consumption, and infrastructure costs like stormwater management.

Green buildings even increase profits. A study of 108 stores in a single national chain, for example, found that stores with skylights and natural daylighting had 40 percent higher sales than stores with little or no daylighting.

The planet benefits in many ways, because green buildings conserve our natural resources, significantly reduce energy consumption, and focus on Earth-friendly alternative energy sources, like photovoltaic panels. They appreciably lower greenhouse gas emissions by, for example, employing HVAC equipment that does not use HCFC, Halon, or CFC-based refrigerants that deplete the ozone and contribute to global warming.

Today, in the US and around the world, every conceivable building type, from offices to schools, warehouses, stores, and homes, is being constructed according to green principles. Hundreds of green buildings have been completed in the US alone, and thousands more are on the drawing board.

Green has gone mainstream

The four-block-long 150,000-square-foot City of Long Beach Maintenance Facility complex, for example, has four separate buildings: a fleet service and office building; the Integrated Resources Bureau office with parking for all of the city's garbage trucks; the Lien Sales and Towing Administration Facility, with parking for more than 1,000 impounded vehicles; a full truck wash; and a police impound facility.

The City of Long Beach told LPA to incorporate green elements into the facility's design only if they did not significantly affect the development schedule or shell budget of $35 per square foot.

So, LPA gave the facility a north–south orientation to bring abundant northern light into the interior without heat gain. In many spaces, in fact, natural light dispersed through windows, horizontal translucent panels, insulated skylights, and roof monitors is the sole interior light source during daytime hours. Reflective roof surfaces reduce the heat island effect.

Recycled materials were used extensively throughout the facility, including recycled laminated glass tops for reception desks and interior signage and panels made from recycled local newspapers. Furniture, carpets, and finish materials were all derived from recycled materials. Concrete removed from the structures originally on the site was broken up and reused as distinctive paving for building entries and courtyards.

Green building principles can be successfully applied to any type of building. The City of Long Beach, California's green Maintenance Facility provides a healthy and attractive workplace, and reduces energy consumption and operational costs.

The U.S. Green Building Council LEEDs the way

The green building movement was born in the mounting concern about the environment of the 1960s, began growing in the energy crisis of the early 1970s, gained momentum in the 1980s with the widespread documentation of sick building syndrome, and began taking its first steps in the 1990s.

The green building movement came into its own with the formation of the U.S. Green Building Council (www.usgbc.org) in 1993. This respected and independent agency—a coalition of organizations from the real estate industry, government, non-profit organizations, and schools—began with approximately 300 members and a determination to represent and advocate green buildings and to create a third-party certification program for green buildings. Now, with nearly 4,000 member organizations, the USGBC is literally changing the built environment in the US and around the world with its LEED program and rating system.

The current version of LEED, launched in 2000, is a demanding program with stringent criteria. It guides the planning and construction of a green building, and then evaluates a facility's performance over its lifecycle, in six categories: sustainable site, water efficiency, energy and atmosphere, materials and resources, indoor environmental quality, and innovation and design process. The LEED rating system has four award levels: Certification (26–32 points), Silver (33–38 points), Gold (39–51 points), and Platinum (52+ points).

One recently developed LEED program—LEED-CI (Commercial Interiors)—is critically important, because it can be applied to the enormous stock of already constructed commercial, retail, and institutional space, much of which will have to be upgraded in coming years to meet new technology and user requirements. With LEED-CI, any future tenant improvement project could, conceivably, be a green project.

In just a few short years, LEED has become the standard for green buildings across the US. LEED criteria for public and even private buildings have been adopted (or adapted) by dozens of US cities (including Austin, Boulder, Chicago, San Diego, San Francisco, and Scottsdale), entire counties from Arlington County in Virginia to Hennepin County in Minnesota, and several state governments including those of California, Maryland, and Pennsylvania.

And yet, as of mid-2005, only approximately 260 buildings had received LEED ratings, and nearly 2,000 buildings had been registered for a LEED rating. Thus, the USGBC created a task force to develop strategies that will bring the USGBC and LEED to a much larger audience and greatly increase the number of green and LEED-rated buildings in the US and around the world.

But even more needs to be done. To become truly mainstream, a critical mass of green buildings must be constructed on standard budgets. Then, every building from a fast food restaurant to a corner gasoline station will be green, and that will have a powerful impact on human health and productivity, energy usage and prices, and a host of environmental issues, from global warming to the leveling of our ancient forests.

A green pioneer

LPA is one of the pioneers of the green building movement. The firm designed a variety of sustainable facilities in the late 1980s and throughout the 1990s that responded to both their climate and context, including the One Venture office building in Irvine, California, the Tucson Gateway Center in Tucson, Arizona, and the Renaissance Center in Las Vegas.

In 1990, LPA was named the AIA California Council Firm of the Year, an award given to one firm in the state that has exhibited design excellence for at least 10 years. One of the jurors noted: "We were particularly impressed with the vernacular and energy efficient approach to the spec developer work which was refreshingly void of the appliqué found in this project type."

In 2000, LPA joined the USGBC and continued its pioneering work:

- LPA designed the first privately developed facility in California to earn a LEED rating: the North American Headquarters for Ford Motor Company's Premier Automotive Group in Irvine (see Chapter 4).

- LPA designed the first privately developed office campus in California—and the largest private facility in the US as of 2003—to receive a LEED Gold rating: the Toyota Motor Sales North American headquarters expansion in Torrance (see Chapter 5).

- LPA designed one of the first true green K–12 schools in California: Cesar Chavez Elementary School, a kindergarten through fifth-grade school for 800 children in downtown Long Beach, California (see Chapter 8).

- LPA's Irvine, California headquarters was a LEED-CI pilot project and one of the first commercial interior projects in California to earn a LEED rating (see Chapter 9).

- LPA even designed two of the first green police stations in the US for the Cities of Cotati and Woodland in California (see Chapter 6).

Left: The green Toyota South Campus expansion in Torrance, California was the largest privately owned Gold LEED certified building in the US upon its completion in 2003. **Above:** The Tucson Gateway Center in Tucson, Arizona was a pioneering green building of the 1990s.

By 2005, LPA had more than 40 LEED-accredited professionals, including its president, Dan Heinfeld, and the firm has completed more LEED-rated buildings than any architectural firm in the state of California.

One of LPA's greatest contributions to the green building movement has been its pioneering mandate that every building, regardless of program, should be green on a mainstream budget. Every sustainable building the firm has designed has been completed on a standard budget, and that is what developers, real estate investors, corporations, and private citizens need to turn our built environment green.

Below: Sunshades above the windows at the Woodland Police Station in Woodland, California, one of the first green police stations in the US, minimize heat gain from direct sunlight. **Right:** Ford Motor Company's Premier Automotive Group headquarters in Irvine, California is a showcase for green architecture, as well as the company's distinctive automobiles.

Debunking the "green costs more" myth

Unfortunately, in the first five years of the new millennium, many green building advocates—including the media—continued to promulgate the "green costs more" myth.

The truth is, green buildings do not have to cost more to construct than their standard counterparts, and sometimes they can even cost less.

It is true that the pioneering green buildings of the 1980s and 1990s were more expensive than standard buildings, because architects and contractors were learning how to create green buildings literally on the job, and their learning curve boosted the project cost. Green building materials, building systems and equipment, and furnishings were also more expensive than those used in standard buildings, and they were often hard to find.

No more.

We now have a critical mass of experience in designing and constructing green buildings. Green buildings are no longer experimental. We know how to create them easily and economically.

Green building materials, systems, fixtures, and furniture are now far cheaper and more widely available than in the 1990s when, for example, a mere 10 percent of building products were made from recycled materials. That figure should grow to 100 percent by 2010.

REQUIRED TO OPERATE A STORE

FOR CONSTRUCTION

GHOUT THE FACILITY

experiment

A raised floor air distribution system, which delivers air at a lower level and uses significantly less energy than the traditional system of forcing air down from the ceiling plenum, was twice as expensive in 1998 as it was in 2003.

Similarly, indirect lighting—which illuminates the ceiling and bounces off the walls, provides a higher light level with less energy and less heat, reduces air conditioning costs, and makes it easier to read—was priced at a premium in 1995, and it was only offered by a few manufacturers. Today, the cost is comparable to standard parabolic lighting, and it is available from a wide variety of manufacturers.

Wal-Mart's experimental sustainable Supercenter in McKinney, Texas demonstrates green building principles to thousands of shoppers every day.

LPA's design for the County of Shasta's 55,000-square-foot Shasta County Library in the City of Redding in northern California incorporated all of those green systems and features—and more—on a mainstream budget. The library has a green roof, energy-generating photovoltaic panels on the south-facing roof, and energy efficient direct and indirect lighting systems with occupancy sensor controls. Approximately 80 percent of the interior receives natural daylight and has outdoor views. Recycled and recyclable materials—including wood, carpeting, and metals—were used extensively throughout the library. Water conservation strategies and drought-tolerant landscaping reduce water consumption by 35 percent compared to a standard public library building. The library also exceeds California's Title 24 energy code, the strictest in the nation, by 22 percent.

But the Shasta County Library goes even further. The library has an HVAC system that generates ice during the night and stores it. The HVAC system then uses that ice during peak summer operating hours—when demands on the energy grid are greatest—to supplement the system's chillers and produce cool air. Thus, the chillers don't have to work as hard or as long, so the system uses less electricity. In addition, a 7,000-square-foot section of the library's roof is landscaped with layers of native California and ornamental grasses and several native and non-native flowering shrubs, including the state flower, the poppy. The landscaped roof diminishes the heat island effect, helps insulate the building (lowering heating and cooling costs), and reduces stormwater runoff from the roof.

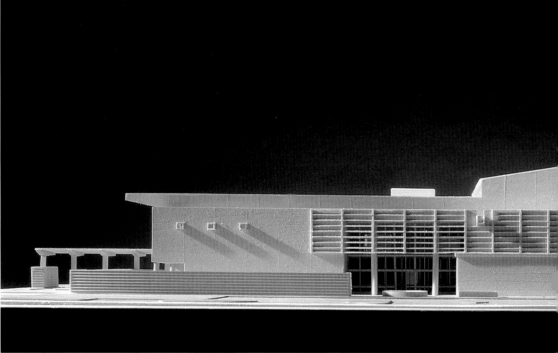

Top left: The City of Redding, California's green Shasta County Public Library has a partial green roof. **Top right:** The dramatic sundial at Southwestern Community College's green Learning Resource Center in Chula Vista, California. **Above:** The City of Redding, California's green Shasta County Public Library.

Green building incentive programs

The cost of green buildings has also gone down thanks to a wide variety of city, state, and federal green building incentive programs, including tax credits for LEED-rated buildings and rebates for energy efficient equipment.

Incentives are everywhere. Seattle, Washington provides reimbursement for energy efficient windows, insulation, refrigeration, pumps, and energy controls in commercial buildings. Arlington County, Virginia awards developers added density or height bonuses if they meet the LEED Silver criteria. The New York State Green Building Tax Credit Program gives tax incentives to commercial developments that incorporate specified green strategies. Idaho provides 4-percent interest loans up to $100,000 for commercial or industrial installation of energy efficient systems. The State of Massachusetts lowers permitting fees by 15 percent (up to $10,000) for LEED-rated buildings.

Many utility companies also provide local incentives, which can help pay for green components. Progress Energy, the utility company for North Carolina, South Carolina, and Florida, for example, provides cash-back incentive programs for the installation of high efficiency HVAC equipment. California's Pacific Gas & Electric, Southern California Edison, and San Diego Gas & Electric have formed a consortium that pays 50 percent of the installation costs for an on-site power system. In addition, Savings by Design, a program sponsored by four of California's largest utilities under the auspices of the Public Utilities Commission, offers incentives to help offset the costs of adding energy efficient building features.

LPA's design for the Southwestern Community College Learning Resource Center in Chula Vista, California, for example, earned a $44,000 Savings by Design energy credit for the community college by incorporating several energy-saving features. These included an energy efficient HVAC system;

a ground floor berm that provides thermal mass cooling and heat conservation; a 60-foot central breezeway that pre-cools air at the building entries; clerestories and an interior "Ventana Del Sol" light well that bring natural daylight deep into the building interior; and exterior metal sunshades that reduce solar heat gain. These features helped the Center exceed California's Title 24 energy requirements by 20 percent.

The green building movement even has some Federal government support. In 2003, the General Services Administration mandated that all new Federal buildings earn a LEED Silver rating.

The green building movement has everything it needs to move fully into the mainstream—improving our lives, our businesses, our schools, and our institutions.

CHAPTER 3

Regardless of a project's budget or its program, LPA believes every building can—and should— be green, and we are proving it in our work every day.

Affordable sustainability is not a new idea for our firm. We have a long track record in designing green buildings on standard budgets.

LPA designed the Irvine Ranch Water District Headquarters, completed in 1988 in Irvine, California, as a model that used architecture, not technology, to demonstrate to the community responsible, energy efficient building design principles that anyone could use. Thus, the building was given a north–south orientation to make the most use of natural daylighting. The south façade is protected by a copper sun screen, and the east and west façades are primarily solid and heavily insulated. The courtyard has a drought-tolerant landscape that uses reclaimed water for all its irrigation needs. In 1988, the headquarters exceeded California's Title 24 energy standards by 50 percent, and it won a Southern California Edison design excellence award.

From the old millennium to the new, LPA continues to design cost-efficient green buildings that serve myriad needs. The 41,500-square-foot Cuyamaca College Student Center in the foothills of El Cajon, California, scheduled for completion in 2007, has a food court and dining facilities, meeting rooms, bookstore, health services, a student lounge, student club rooms, and a host of green features from natural daylighting to reclaimed irrigation water and large roof overhangs that shield the windows and collect and scrub rainwater from the roof before releasing it back into the groundwater system. All of this, and more, was done on the typical budget for university facilities provided by the State of California.

What does it take to design and build green on a mainstream budget?

GREEN GOES MAINSTREAM
BY DAN HEINFELD, FAIA PRESIDENT, LPA, INC.

The green Irvine Ranch Water District headquarters in Irvine, California has an architecturally dramatic window sunshade that also reduces glare and interior solar heat gain.

The green planning and design process

Green is not a gimmick that gets overlaid on a project at the end of the planning or design process, like an architectural cosmetic feature. It must be integrated into each project at the beginning of the planning and design process to make sustainability part of a building's DNA.

Collaboration and communication are the foundation of the green development process. Team members, including developer/owner, client, architect, outside consultants, and contractor, work together from the very start of the design process. When LPA designed the Shasta County Library in Redding, California, for example, we collaborated from the beginning with representatives from the local library committee, the town government, the County of Shasta, and even the State of California (the library was primarily funded by a state bond act), as well as the project's engineering team and consultants.

Through collaboration, LPA brought together the disparate needs and concerns of the project team into a single, cohesive design. Redding's citizens, government, and the local library committee wanted a design that was sustainable, provided outdoor views, had abundant natural light, and emphasized local history and architecture. The County and State focused mainly on function, including reduced operating and maintenance costs, and budget. All design issues were discussed within the team, and all of the representatives had to agree on the resolution of each design issue.

With a collaborative framework in place, the green development process begins by looking at the entire project—site, exterior, interior, and budget—as a whole before planning or designing a single element. This holistic view of the building shows the design team how the many elements are connected and how they can work together to create the best sustainable development within the project budget.

Thus, from the outset, the team can manage the critical interplay of each green component with the rest of the building.

An Energy Star roof, for example, reflects sunlight, bouncing heat off and away from a building. The engineer must know that, instead of the normal 20 degrees of heat that migrate through a standard roof, only 5 degrees of heat migrate through an Energy Star roof. So, the roof should be engineered in the 90 degree range, not in the 110 or 120 degree range. The reduced heat exchange, in turn, lowers the HVAC requirements and decreases the amount of insulation needed in the building. The money saved from the basic decision to have an Energy Star roof can then be used for other green features and design opportunities.

Looking at a building as one complex interconnected system gives the architectural team a very powerful design tool. No longer does the architect merely address the "six-inch" face of the exterior while the engineer plans the structural, mechanical, and electrical systems. The architect is now the leader of a collaborative green team searching for holistic approaches to the entire building design, structure, and systems.

With a collaborative green development process, the team can also alter up front planning and design elements and shift budget allocations from one building component to another to meet the larger project objectives of a cost-effective green building. For example, the team could choose to forego a costly and environmentally insignificant feature—such as a showy lobby—to set aside more of the budget for important green strategies like a displacement ventilation system or even a green (garden) roof, both of which will significantly reduce the building's air conditioning use and its energy bills, particularly in the summer.

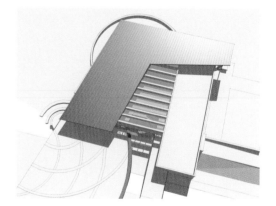

The green Student Center at Cuyamaca College in El Cajon, California is nestled into its hillside setting to minimize its visual intrusion on the landscape, preserve view corridors, and help keep the building cool in hot weather.

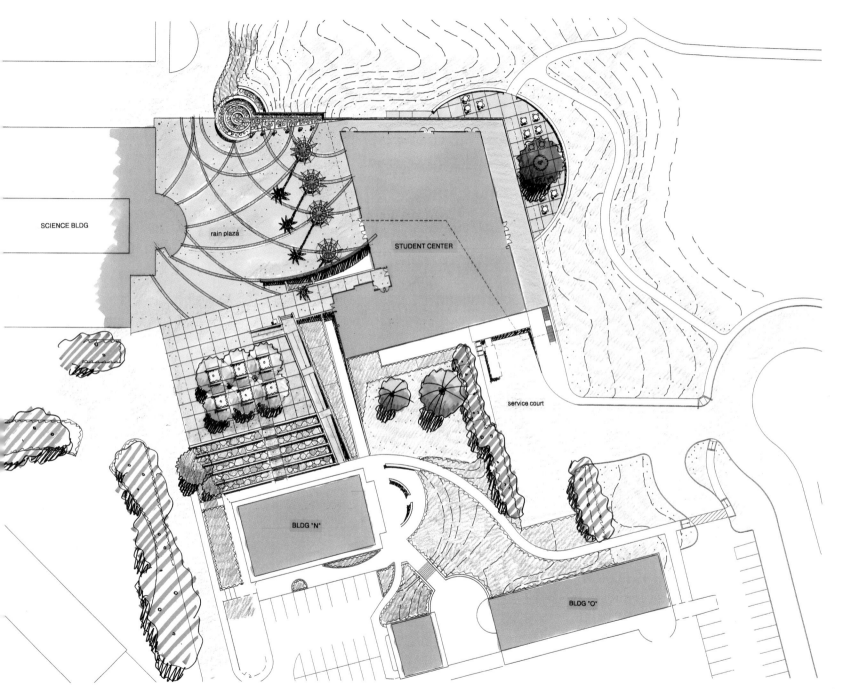

SCIENCE BLDG

rain plaza

STUDENT CENTER

service court

BLDG "N"

BLDG "O"

27

Some basic green budget strategies

Site planning is one of the most cost-effective ways to turn a facility green. Buildings can be oriented to reduce the creation of heat islands, which will lower HVAC costs. Building orientation can also maximize solar exposure to support the use of photovoltaic panels to generate electricity.

In the case of the new Student Center for Cuyamaca College in the hot and arid foothills of El Cajon, California, LPA set the centrally located two-story building into a hill. This helps maintain the view corridors to the valley for the adjacent buildings while minimizing the Center's western exposure, which reduces heat gain. The north and east sides of the building are oriented to bring natural daylighting into the Student Center. This orientation, plus a roofed exterior deck and the shade cast by the building, also helps cool the air and supports not only natural ventilation but also comfortable outdoor seating areas.

A green site plan should focus, in particular, on minimizing the development footprint. When less land is used by buildings, roads, and parking, fewer stormwater management systems are required, and more land is available for open space. This lowers project costs and enhances property value while also supporting wildlife habitat.

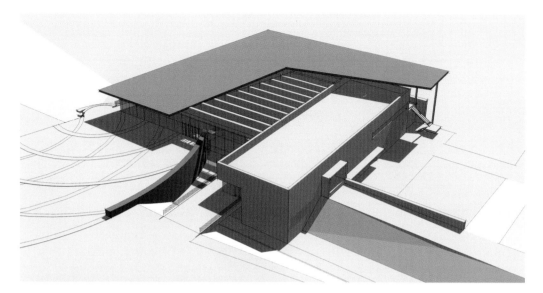

The green Student Center at Cuyamaca College in El Cajon, California.

Landscape architecture—the use of trees, flowers, shrubs, hedges, and native grasses—is one of the most important and cost-effective tools for creating a green facility.

First, landscape architecture can significantly reduce heat islands, which will lower HVAC requirements and costs. A green screen—a metal lattice planted with vines and/or climbing flowers—along a building's western façade will limit heat absorption. Placing trees along the south façade of a building will provide both shade and heat reduction in the summer. Selecting deciduous trees that drop their leaves every fall will allow the facility to enjoy warmth and sunlight during the cold winter months, which will reduce energy usage and heating bills.

Trees and arbors planted around (and throughout) a parking lot minimize heat islands and create a shaded, attractive, even welcoming parking area. Trees, which absorb air pollution, can also be used to significantly improve air quality, an important LEED requirement.

Second, in regions where water is a limited commodity, the use of drought-tolerant and native plants will conserve water, reduce maintenance costs, and beautify the property. LPA's master plan for the 147-acre Las Positas College in Livermore, California includes a xeriscape landscape plan with drought-tolerant native trees and shrubs. The playing surfaces of the soccer, baseball, and softball fields have synthetic turf, which requires no irrigation.

The use of drought-tolerant native plant species is an important green design element at the sustainable Toyota South Campus expansion in Torrance, California.

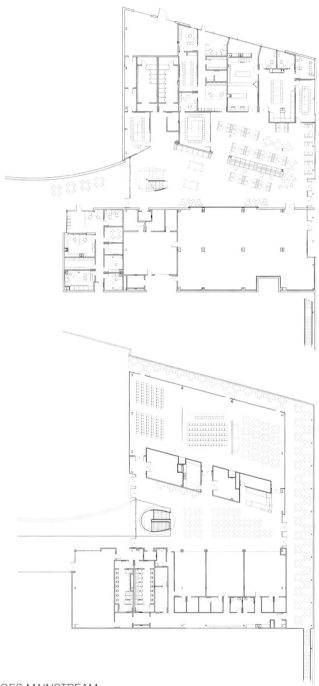

Third, on large properties like an office or college campus, the site's open space can be used to cost-effectively meet stormwater management requirements. The Las Positas College master plan includes bioswales and a system of backfilling sub-grade detention areas—ponds—to capture and cleanse runoff. A pervious paving system is used in parking areas where surface gradients allow, which enables the ground to absorb stormwater, helping to recharge the groundwater aquifers.

Interior planning—floor layout and usage—is another cost-effective means of turning a building green. Long, narrow floorplates, for example, maximize the use of natural daylighting, which lessens the need for artificial illumination, reduces energy consumption, minimizes heat gain from artificial lighting, and lowers air conditioning use. Most pre-Second World War office buildings—from Chicago's first skyscrapers to the original Rockefeller Center towers in New York—were designed so that tenant spaces would have natural light, as well as good ventilation.

Placing fixed elements like stairs, mechanical systems, kitchens, and bathrooms in the middle of a floorplate and leaving the perimeter open helps to bring natural daylighting to everyone on that floor.

LPA's interior layout for the Cuyamaca College Student Center places all the utility functions along the west and south walls to minimize building openings and heat gain. The Center's main public spaces are arranged along the east and north walls, which have floor-to-ceiling glass that brings in abundant natural daylighting. The central dining room has a skylight and clerestory windows that bring natural daylight into the building interior.

An interior floorplan can help a building achieve many green objectives. LPA's interior layout for the Cuyamaca College Student Center in El Cajon, California places all the utility functions along the west and south walls to minimize building openings and heat gain. The Center's main public spaces are arranged along the east and north walls, which have floor-to-ceiling glass that brings in abundant natural daylighting.

Stormwater management is an important green strategy in every region. Wal-Mart's experimental sustainable Supercenter in McKinney, Texas uses a variety of stormwater management strategies, including permeable paving, landscaping, bioswales, and a stormwater retention pond.

Green is beautiful

The green development process not only creates a cost-effective sustainable building—it also creates an architectural design that will stand the test of time.

Sustainability and good design go hand-in-hand. Tried and true architectural principles like good solar orientation—coupled with the improving sustainable design technology marketplace—give an architect a great foundation on which to base real architecture.

LPA does not chase after architectural fashion or the fad of the moment; we believe architecture is too important to be based on current styles.

The firm focuses instead on creating timeless architecture, rooted in place, that takes advantage of the new sustainable technologies, is functional and flexible, and generates long-term value.

For LPA, place is comprised of climate, landscape, and the regional architecture. As the architect Vitruvius wrote in the first century BC: "We must begin by taking note of the countries and climates in which homes are to be built if our designs for them are to be correct. One type of house seems appropriate for Egypt, another for Spain... one still different for Rome... It is obvious that design for homes ought to conform to diversities of climate." Or, to bring that theory to the United States: Florida's historic architecture and its use of local materials and passive heating and cooling design in response to its climate and landscape makes its buildings look different from those of Arizona. They have a unique appearance and character. They create a sense of place because their architecture reflects their place.

LPA's sustainable buildings take the time-honored architectural traditions of a particular place and interpret them for our time. We understand how traditional architecture was trying to respond to its place. We then look for ways to combine historic architectural design with sustainable design and the advanced design understanding and technologies of today to create our own traditions, a new aesthetic that responds to the needs of this time and is sympathetic and contextual to its place.

Think of the thick adobe walls of the sun-drenched Southwest, which used thermal lag to keep a building cool in the daytime and warm at night. Adobe construction is much too costly to re-create today, but we can use the principal of thermal lag when designing a building. LPA's design for Wal-Mart's experimental and environmentally responsible supercenter in Aurora, Colorado, for example, includes a solar wall that functions in the same way as the thick mass of an adobe wall: it has heat-absorbing material and a space that works with the ventilation system to move air in and out of the building. The solar wall heats the warehouse in the winter and keeps the space cool in the summer.

At LPA, we believe that understanding and looking again to time-honored principles of designing for place, and giving them a modern interpretation, forms the basis for an authentic architecture that, when coupled with the sustainable technologies available today, can create an architecture that is beautiful and will stand the test of time, because it is based on climate, landscape, and real needs.

The Irvine Ranch Water District Headquarters in Irvine, California, which was completed in 1988, still looks fresh and new today, because LPA's sustainable architectural design is a reflection of the building's place, not fashion. The patina of the natural local materials of copper and limestone give the headquarters a sense of permanence. The courtyard is part of a centuries-old Southern California architectural tradition, and it also brings daylight into the deepest interior spaces. The drought-tolerant landscaping and water features cool the courtyard and reduce heat gain for the entire building. The north–south orientation of the office wing floods the interior with natural light, while a copper louver system on the south façade protects the interior from solar heat gain.

We believe that any building can be green, cost-effective, and beautiful. All of the following building projects in this book prove that point: each has won an American Institute of Architects design award, and each one is a sustainable project completed on a mainstream budget.

A side view of the environmentally responsible Chancellor's Building for California State University (CSU) at Long Beach shows the sunshades that reduce heat gain and glare from south-facing windows, while preserving views.

33

MainstreamGreen

SustainableDesignByLPA SelectedProjects

The Ford Motor Company's Premier Automotive Group North American Headquarters is a 310,000-square-foot facility, located in the Irvine Spectrum Center in the City of Irvine, 40 miles south of downtown Los Angeles. It was the first privately developed facility in California—and one of the largest private facilities in the US—to receive LEED certification from the U.S. Green Building Council in 2001.

Choosing green

In 1998, the Ford Motor Company decided to bring together for the first time all five of its luxury brands—Aston Martin, Jaguar, Land Rover, Lincoln, and Volvo—under one umbrella. The Premier Automotive Group was established as an identifiable and united entity in the marketplace, creating synergies between the five brands in investment, engineering, marketing, and distribution.

Ford also wanted to bring the national headquarters for its luxury brands together physically under one roof. So, in 1999, it decided to construct a Premier Automotive Group North American Headquarters building in the world's largest luxury market—Southern California—to mount a stronger challenge to rival brands in this highly competitive marketplace. Ford chose the 11.9-acre Irvine, California site because of its centralized Southern California location.

From the beginning, the Premier Automotive Group headquarters was planned as a green facility to support Ford's corporate mission and global future. The green orientation was also championed by Ford CEO and Chairman William Clay Ford, Jr., a committed environmentalist.

Green marketplace objectives

The Ford Motor Company had several objectives for the Premier Automotive Group new North American Headquarters that it wanted incorporated into the facility's design:

- Demonstrate Ford Motor Company's commitment to the environment by showcasing intelligent, sustainable building design.

- Provide a superior work environment for all employees that also immerses them in the competitive Southern California luxury automobile market.

- Create a design that consolidates the luxury subsidiaries under one roof, builds synergies between the brands, and maximizes efficiency, while also maintaining and strengthening the individual brand identities.

PREMIER AUTOMOTIVE GROUP NORTH AMERICAN HEADQUARTERS
IRVINE, CALIFORNIA

Building green

The 11.9-acre site has a 153,606-square-foot, five-story office building with an additional one-story 77,122-square-foot Product Development wing, a four-story parking structure, 268 surface parking spaces, and 3 acres (25 percent of the site) of usable open space.

Some of the building components that earned the headquarters' LEED certification include:

- A 200-kilowatt natural gas fuel cell system provides 25 percent of the headquarters' power and hot water.

- The raised floor air distribution system is 30 percent more efficient than a typical top down forced air system.

- Restrooms are equipped with low flow infrared toilets and sinks.

- Reclaimed water is provided by a municipal recycling system for all irrigation and flushing plumbing fixtures on the headquarters site.

- An open office floorplan and glass-enclosed perimeter offices give more than 90 percent of the 800 employees outdoor views and natural daylighting.

- The artificial lighting system includes indirect lighting in office areas, energy efficient light bulbs, and T-5 lamps. A control system automatically dims perimeter lights when daylighting is adequate to properly illuminate the space, saving energy and operating costs.

- The light, reflective color of the Energy Star roof on the office building reduces both the heat island effects on the site and heat absorption of a darker roof surface, lowering air conditioning needs and costs.

- Drought-tolerant landscape.

- 30,000 square feet of the Product Development wing's roof have been landscaped with more than 30 different native plant species, which significantly reduces heat islands on the site. The rooftop landscaping uses rain water for drip irrigation, requires 67 percent less water than standard campus landscaping, helps insulate the upper floors of the wing, saves on future roofing costs, and provides increased energy efficiency. The rooftop landscaping also serves as a bird sanctuary.

- Green screens on the exterior of the Product Development wing, the freeway side of the office building, and the freeway side of the parking structure shade the walls and top floors, and provide insulation for the interior spaces.

- Building and furnishing materials, finishes, and furniture have 30 percent recycled content.

- The headquarters has a four-story parking structure and 268 surface parking spaces. Surface lots were kept to a minimum to reduce the amount of hard surfaces and heat islands on campus, and to maximize open space and landscape opportunities.

- The headquarters has 35 electrical vehicle charging stations, bicycle storage and showers, and direct connections to local bus lines and the Metrolink commuter rail system.

By going green, the Premier Automotive Group headquarters exceeds California's Title 24 energy requirements, which are the strictest in the nation, by more than 25 percent. That, coupled with the fuel cell system, which provides approximately 25 percent of the buildings' overall power, reduces reliance on the local power grid by 50 percent, and therefore reduces operations costs.

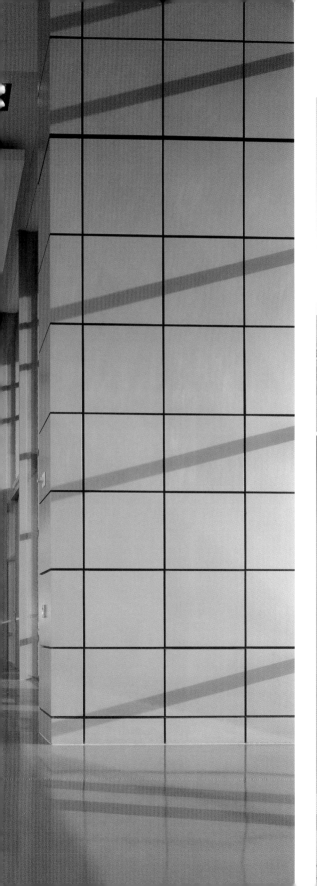

A challenging project

LPA had to surmount several challenges in designing the Premier Automotive Group's headquarters as a green facility with a striking corporate presence. The long, linear, narrow site did not provide the optimum sustainable building orientation or configuration for a facility of this size and magnitude. In addition, the Irvine Spectrum area's specific design guidelines restricted the use of traditional solar control devices, which are not among the vast business park's approved design elements.

Different sides of the property also bordered very different developments. The east side of the site faced a freeway and office and retail developments. The west side of the site overlooked Gateway Boulevard, which connects directly to the region's largest entertainment center.

LPA's biggest challenge, however, was not green design but consolidating five very distinct brands within a unified Premier Automotive Group framework while using design to express each brand's individual identity.

LPA responded to these challenges in several ways.

The main office tower, Product Development wing, and parking structure have two different façades. The freeway-facing building façades were designed to fit within Irvine Spectrum's design guidelines requirements and overall aesthetic through the use of precast concrete, punched openings, and an orthogonal frame. Metal fins create a 30-foot rhythm along the freeway and are used to attach a series of accessories—including shading devices and green screens—that soften the façades.

The building façades facing Gateway Boulevard provide the formal entries into the buildings. LPA selected materials for the main office building façade that are used in the automotive industry: glass and recycled aluminum panels in the branded Premier Automotive Group color, a dark champagne metallic. The exterior design is also based on the automobile. The striking curved metal and glass façade borrows its soft form and shape from elements found in each of the five Premier brands. The pattern of the glass, metal, and concrete façade, for example, mimics Lincoln's vertical front grille design and Land Rover's horizontal grille.

The Gateway façade of the Product Development wing does not have the broad glass bands of the main office tower, for security reasons. Instead, high clerestory glass protected by a metal louver system runs in a broad horizontal strip along the top of the façade, providing both security and natural light for the interior.

A green screen surrounds both the four-story, 633-stall parking structure and the Product Development wing, shading them and blending these buildings into the headquarters landscape. That screening, in turn, enables the main office building to become the dominant feature on the site.

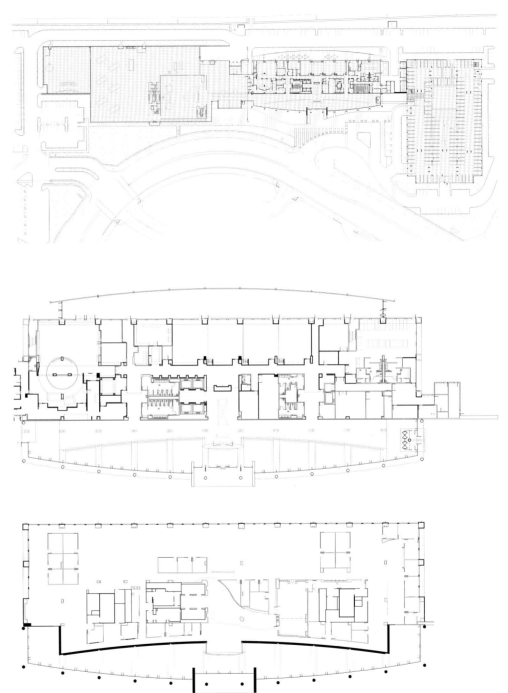

Branding the interior

The interior was designed to showcase the vehicles on display and to support the identity of the different brands. Thus, the common areas of the building use the Premier Automotive Group's dark champagne metallic color palette, which provides a neutral backdrop for each of the five distinct brands. The 37,000-square-foot floors for each of the Premier Automotive Group brands, however, were designed to reflect the individual style, personality, operations, and people of each brand, while also incorporating features that refer to the overall Premier Automotive Group identity.

First Floor: A two-story 13,000-square-foot lobby spans the entire front of the building. The convex curve of the 250-foot-long lobby, which is used as an exhibition area for the different automotive brands, plays off the façade's clear glass. A floating mural depicts the history and future of each of the five automotive brands.

The first floor also has a 4,400-square-foot full-service conference center that can hold up to 250 people and can also be divided into four discrete meeting rooms. A separate multimedia room provides state-of-the-art conferencing services, including video conferencing. The first floor also has four additional breakout meeting rooms with a neutral design for use by all brands.

Employee amenities on this floor include a 3,500-square-foot, state-of-the-art fitness center, the 105-seat Premier Café, which also has two executive dining rooms, and a multicultural room celebrating employees' heritages.

Second Floor—Aston Martin and Jaguar: The voluptuous curves of the sea-green glass walls, reception desk, and coffee bar reflect the sensual lines of these British-born automobiles. LPA selected colors, materials, furnishings, and form to reflect the curvilinear character of the Jaguar brand and the hand-crafted detailing of the understated Aston Martin brand.

Third Floor—Volvo: The spacious lobby of light wood and Volvo's signature blue reflects the brand's Scandinavian heritage. The lobby's open design and exterior glass walls and the crisp, clean contemporary style throughout the third floor represent Volvo's distinct design philosophy. This floor has photographic displays, a coffee bar, and a main conference room.

Fourth Floor—Lincoln Mercury: LPA designed a split configuration of rich earth tones with dramatic splashes of color that allows both brands to make a distinctive statement within a singular environment. In the lobby, for example, limestone used on a "runway" and the reception desk reflects Lincoln's "American luxury" character, while the detailing and choice of color and materials complements the Mercury palette.

Fifth Floor—Land Rover and the Premier Automotive Group: The lobby's wood floor, sisal rugs, and stone reception desk reflect the cross-country orientation of Land Rover, and its sophistication. The floor also has a seating area around a large-format plasma screen, a large retail display wall, and a conference center.

Product Development Wing: The interior of this single-story, 77,000-square-foot design studio has a mezzanine, an exposed ceiling, and a more high-tech design than the main office building. The interior focus is on flexible, moveable spaces that support the different and changeable project teams and work groups.

The wing has a 10,000-square-foot product showroom with three vehicle display turntables, six projectors, audiovisual systems, and an elaborate lighting system that mimics dawn to dusk lighting. The showroom displays prototypes and new models from each of the brands and also allows designers to study vehicle models more closely.

A clay automobile model studio opens into a working courtyard with a turntable on which clay models can be studied in the sunlight. The wing also has office space for 85 design employees, a paint booth, wood and metal fabricating areas, and a vehicle tear-down area.

The Premier Automotive Group wanted an architectural design for this wing that brought in considerable natural sunlight while providing product security. A 25-foot-high wall prevents views into the courtyard. Solid walls with clerestory windows at the top also mitigate views, provide privacy, and bring in plentiful sunlight.

Green construction

Construction of the Premier Automotive Group's North American Headquarters began in May 2000. Employees moved into the new headquarters in November 2001. Construction was completed in January 2002.

LEED has criteria for construction waste management that diverts material from landfills. Thus, 60 percent of the Premier Automotive Group's construction waste was recycled. Other measures included completing construction operations prior to enclosing the major portions of the building and starting the HVAC systems to minimize off-gassing from the building materials.

With all of the many green features and design components incorporated into the Premier Automotive Group's new headquarters, the project still met Ford's budget of less than $100 per square foot, and Ford will enjoy reduced operating costs every year over the life of the buildings.

Project: Premier Automotive Group North American Headquarters
Location: Irvine, California
Size: 310,000 square feet
Construction cost: $68 million

Green features:

- A 200-kilowatt natural gas fuel cell system that provides 25 percent of the headquarters' power and hot water.
- A raised floor air distribution system that is 30 percent more efficient than a typical top down forced air system.
- Exceeds California's Title 24 energy requirements by more than 25 percent.
- Reliance on the local power grid reduced by 50 percent.
- Restrooms are equipped with low flow infrared toilets and sinks.
- Reclaimed water for all irrigation and flushing plumbing fixtures.
- More than 90 percent of the 800 employees have outdoor views and natural daylighting.
- The artificial lighting system includes indirect lighting and a control system that automatically dims perimeter lights when daylighting is adequate to properly illuminate the space.
- Energy Star roof on the office building.
- Landscaped roof over the majority of the Product Development wing.
- Drought-tolerant landscape.
- Green screens shade the walls and top floors, and provide insulation for the interior spaces.
- Building and furnishing materials and finishes have 30 percent recycled content.
- 35 electrical vehicle charging stations, bicycle storage and showers, and direct connections to local bus lines and the Metrolink commuter rail system.

CHAPTER 5

The 624,000-square-foot South Campus Office Development expansion of the 135-acre North American headquarters of Toyota Motor Sales (TMS) in Torrance, California, was the first privately developed office campus in California—and the largest facility in the US—to receive a LEED Gold rating when it was completed in 2003.

Toyota had wanted to earn a LEED rating, but the company didn't want to use a gold-plated budget to get it. The project had to cost less than the average office space lease Toyota was already paying for rental space in Torrance in the mid-1990s. Those office leases were running in the mid-to-high $20 per square foot range at that time.

By meeting the rigorous LEED requirements within that tight budget, LPA and Toyota flouted the then-conventional wisdom that green buildings must cost more to construct than standard buildings.

TOYOTA MOTOR SALES USA, INC. NORTH AMERICAN HEADQUARTERS, SOUTH CAMPUS EXPANSION
TORRANCE, CALIFORNIA

Toyota's goals

In addition to earning a LEED rating, Toyota had several other objectives for the South Campus, starting with consolidation.

Toyota's Customer Services Division and the Toyota Financial Services' main office occupied several leased buildings in Torrance, California, separate from the headquarters location. The company wanted to bring together all 2,500 of its Torrance-based employees on one campus. The South Campus expansion allowed Toyota to centralize its operations and, at the same time, integrate its corporate philosophy—which emphasizes worker comfort, efficiency, and social and environmental values—into a high-quality office facility.

Finally, Toyota wanted outdoor meeting space for presentations to Toyota associates and for special events.

In 1996, LPA was engaged by Toyota to master plan the vacant 40-acre South Campus expansion site within its 135-acre headquarters campus and create an overall framework for future development. The project broke ground in September 2001. Move-in was completed in March 2003.

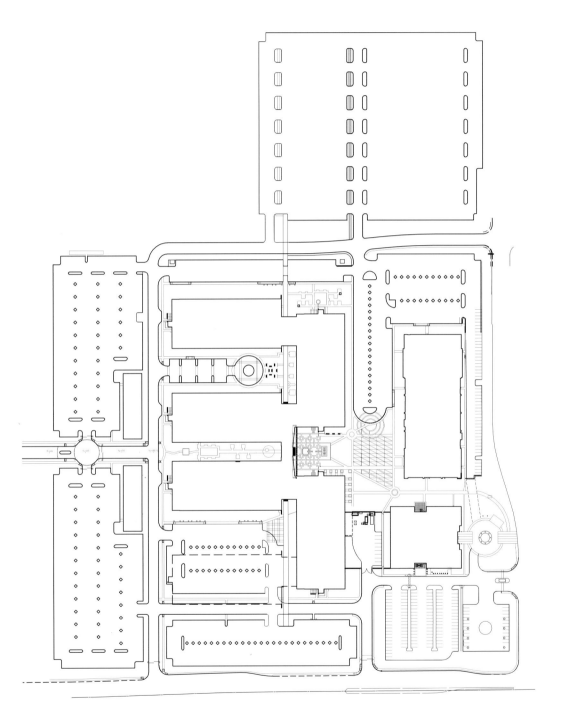

Planning challenges

In addition to going green within Toyota's strict financial limitations, LPA faced a variety of other project challenges. The firm, for example, had to master plan and design the South Campus according to LEED guidelines when the LEED program was in its infancy. That meant going into planning and design areas that were largely unknown, implementing new and innovative technology and strategies that had never been tried before, and meeting both Toyota's move-in schedule and the rigorous LEED requirements.

The 40-acre South Campus site itself also posed several challenges. Major SCE (Southern California Edison) electrical transmission lines had to be relocated. Design and exterior material choices had to minimize the impact of soot from oil refineries west of the site that falls on the South Campus. Railroad tracks had to be removed and oil pipelines moved to make room for a regional storm drain. Landscape construction had to be adapted to the site's shallow storm drain and the soil's very high clay content, which made site drainage and the use of drought-tolerant plants difficult.

Upon project completion, LPA had created 624,000 gross square feet of office space in two three-story office buildings with a total of five "pods," or sections. The Toyota Financial Services building has three distinct sections connected by lobbies. The Customer Services building—parallel to the Toyota Financial Services building—has two distinct sections. The two main buildings are connected by a long common lobby.

The South Campus also has 2,339 surface parking spaces, a pedestrian circulation loop, and more than 8 acres of landscaped open space, including an outdoor seating area for the employee dining center, break-out rooms, a jogging trail, and an outdoor stage. Two lots were set aside for future development.

Green features

To earn a LEED rating, LPA and Toyota planned all building elements to meet or surpass key LEED criteria. The South Campus' energy performance, for example, exceeds both the California Title 24 energy code and the minimum LEED requirements by more than 42 percent, thanks to features like the rooftop solar electric system—the largest of its type in North America—a renewable resource that provides 20 percent of the buildings' energy requirements.

A wide variety of green building materials and furnishings were incorporated into the campus. More than 50 percent (by value) of the building materials have recycled content. The gypsum board walls, for example, have 15 percent recycled content, and the structural steel system has 100 percent recycled content.

None of the HVAC, fire suppression, and refrigeration equipment use ozone-depleting hydrochlorofluorocarbon (HCFC), Halon, or chlorofluorocarbon (CFC)-based refrigerants. The ductwork has special Mylar lining that is more easily cleaned and does not release fibers into the indoor or outdoor environments. Copy rooms and janitorial facilities are set within separate floor-to-ceiling walls and have their own ventilation systems to isolate chemical contaminants and keep them from affecting the indoor air quality in the office areas.

To further reduce potential air quality contaminants and irritants, LPA selected paints and adhesives that meet the strict volatile organic compound (VOC) limits set by the South Coast Air Quality Management District. Composite wood products free of urea-formaldehyde resins were used, and carpeting meets or exceeds the Carpet and Rug Institute's Green Label Indoor Air Quality Test Program.

Water conservation was a critical planning component. Each South Campus building was designed to connect flushing plumbing fixtures as well as cooling towers in the central plant to a recycled water system that Toyota was extending throughout its entire 135-acre headquarters campus. Low flow plumbing fixtures reduced building water usage by more than 20 percent.

Pedestrian and vehicular circulation systems required green planning and design, because they have a direct impact on sustainability and the environment.

The South Campus circulation system separates pedestrian and vehicular traffic, and further separates deliveries and recycling pick-up routes from the rest of the campus traffic. A pedestrian circulation system integrated into the campus-wide landscape design encourages walking rather than short car trips between different campus buildings. The circulation system was also designed to strengthen the South Campus' direct relationships with the rest of the Toyota campus. A jogging trail, for example, was extended into and through the South Campus to create a campus-wide loop. The connection node—with its turf, flowering canopy trees, and sequoias—also provides clear, direct pedestrian links to the main campus.

To further reduce the use of fossil fuels to, from, and on campus, and to support employee use of alternative transportation, the South Campus has electric vehicle shuttles to off-site public transportation systems, bicycle racks for more than 100 bicycles, showers for cyclists to promote bicycle use.

LPA made its South Campus landscape architecture plan one of the most important features of the overall site plan. The landscape design, for example, incorporates a variety of usable outdoor spaces, which enable Toyota associates to take typical indoor functions outside into the landscape, and which also help unite the northern and southern portions of the campus into a user-friendly whole. The perimeter landscaping was designed to provide Toyota with a secure edge, blend with the surrounding environment, and present a friendly face to the community. A hedge was used rather than a fence on the site's most public side.

Landscape architecture also supports Toyota's green objectives. Buildings and the surface parking lots are heavily landscaped with trees to provide shade for pedestrians, minimize heat islands, and help clean the air. The campus-wide drip irrigation system uses reclaimed rather than potable water which, coupled with the high use of drought-tolerant plant and tree species, reduces landscape water usage by more than 50 percent.

In 2005, the South Campus received the prestigious Honor Award from the American Society of Landscape Architects (ASLA) in the category of Multi-Discipline Design.

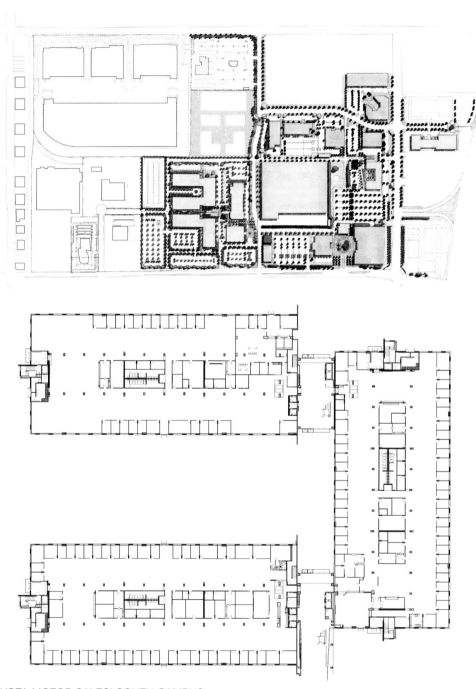

Architectural design

LPA's exterior design principles focused on integrating the South Campus buildings into the already established architectural context of the existing headquarters campus. The building mass was shaped in response to the site's solar orientation to maximize interior daylighting and also reduce heat gain.

To minimize construction costs and free up additional money for green features, concrete tilt-up walls were used for all the buildings. A number of design features were used to avoid the typical tilt-up look of rows of punched windows in a smooth concrete façade that says "low budget." The appearance of attractive banded horizontal windows, for example, was created by putting a piece of handsomely frosted glass (or fritting) between pairs of punched windows to conceal the structural concrete wall between the two openings and create the more stylish horizontal banded look.

Green considerations also shaped the design of the building exteriors. The windows on the south side of the buildings—which receive constant sunlight, including infrared rays (heat)—are glazed with Low-E glass and are slightly inset into the concrete wall to provide greater interior shade and lessen interior heat build-up, which reduces energy usage. The windows on the other three sides of the buildings, which do not have the same light and heat problems, are flush with the concrete walls.

LPA's interior design was guided by three principles:

- To support Toyota's commitment to continuous improvement, or "Kaizen," which includes the constant evolution of its business units. Thus, the interior design had to support changes in the future.

- To support Toyota's commitment to the environment, including working closely with manufacturers to raise the "green bar" on sustainable materials and finishes to enhance indoor air quality and support the planet as a whole.

- To support and promote access to and connection between Toyota business units that once worked separately in different buildings in Torrance.

To encourage employee interaction, a two-story light-filled common lobby with a Bavarian limestone floor connects the two main buildings. A series of smaller, horizontal ground-floor lobbies connect the different sections of each building to each other and serve as gathering places for employees and executives, which promotes formal and informal conversations. In addition to elevators, lobby-based glass stairwells provide vertical circulation and also act as extensions of the office floorplates, encouraging floor-to-floor interactions.

The floorplan for each of the five building sections was designed around a central core that has restrooms, business centers, file/storage rooms, copy rooms, break areas, and designated recycling areas. Beyond the central core are open floorplan office areas with open workstations that can be easily moved or reconfigured to meet the changing needs of each business unit.

The perimeter of each floorplate is ringed with glass-enclosed private offices that allow natural daylight to pass from the exterior to the interior of the floors. The office floors have 9-foot-6-inch ceilings (rather than the standard 9-foot ceilings) that provide greater openness and better natural lighting. Thus, more than 90 percent of the workers enjoy outdoor views and natural daylight, an important component of sustainable architecture and employee well-being.

Environmentally responsible construction processes

The LEED rating criteria include the actual construction process. Turner Construction Company of Irvine, California, the project's general contractor, implemented a waste management program that recycled close to 90 percent of the South Campus' construction waste. The buildings' concrete tilt-up wall molds, for example, were reused in hardscape features, like sidewalks. To prevent construction from creating air quality problems in the surrounding area, pollutant sources were controlled by sealing mechanical ductwork in the shop before installing it, and keeping the ducts sealed until they were connected. Coordinated construction sequencing of wet and dry activities was used to avoid contaminating dry materials that would absorb moisture and become a breeding ground for mold or bacteria growth.

To safeguard indoor air quality, the HVAC systems were protected from contamination during construction and proper housekeeping schedules were enforced. Post-construction flushing of the HVAC systems and ductwork removed construction dust and debris left over from the original manufacturing process to further assure a superior indoor air quality.

On Earth Day—April 22—in 2003, the South Campus received its LEED Gold rating from the USGBC. LPA and Toyota had proven to every major company around the world that they, too, could go green on a mainstream budget. The project subsequently received favorable press coverage in the *Los Angeles Times* and *The New York Times*, and on television on the *Jim Lehrer News Hour* on PBS.

Project: Toyota Motor Sales' North American Headquarters South Campus Office Development Expansion

Location: Torrance, California

Size: 624,000 square feet

Construction cost: $82 million

Green features:

- Energy performance exceeds both the California Title 24 energy code and the minimum LEED requirements by more than 42 percent.
- Single largest commercial solar rooftop electric system in North America provides 20 percent of the buildings' energy requirements.
- More than 50 percent (by value) of the building materials have recycled content.
- None of the HVAC, fire suppression, and refrigeration equipment use ozone-depleting hydrochlorofluorocarbon (HCFC), Halon, or chlorofluorocarbon (CFC)-based refrigerants.
- Copy rooms and janitorial facilities have their own ventilation systems.
- Low-VOC paints, adhesives, and composite wood products.
- Low-flow plumbing fixtures reduced building water usage by more than 20 percent.
- High use of drought-tolerant plant and tree species.
- Buildings and the surface parking lots are heavily landscaped with trees to minimize heat islands.
- Campus-wide drip irrigation system uses reclaimed rather than potable water.
- Landscape water usage reduced by more than 50 percent.
- Pedestrian circulation system encourages walking rather than short car trips between different campus buildings.
- Electric vehicle shuttles to off-site public transportation systems, bicycle racks for more than 100 bicycles, and showers for cyclists.

CHAPTER 6

The media has reported on green office buildings, green schools, green stores, and green libraries, but who'd have ever thought a police station could go green?

The City of Woodland, California did think it, and built it through a competition. LPA won the contract to design the new facility by making the sustainable features an integrated planning and design element of the overall project. In fact, the City of Woodland, California's 52,300-square-foot police station is one of the first green police stations in the US to qualify for LEED certification.

The City of Woodland

Woodland, California was founded in 1853 and incorporated in 1871. It is the county seat of Yolo County in California's Central Valley. Woodland is located 20 miles northwest of Sacramento.

In the late 1990s, Woodland was redeveloping its 27-acre downtown railyard, two blocks from the city's historic downtown core. Known as the Gateway Revitalization Area, the redevelopment was planned with a mix of new uses: apartments, stores, offices, and civic buildings, including the new police station, which the City hoped would create an image of increased safety for the project area and also provide customers for the new uses.

CITY OF WOODLAND
POLICE STATION
WOODLAND,
CALIFORNIA

The City wanted its police station to:

- Consolidate the police department's 101 employees, who were spread among several facilities, onto a single site.

- Replace the existing inefficient police station with a new facility that would enhance the department's operational effectiveness and reduce potential liabilities.

- Be a flexible facility that would support the Police Department's growing needs—including future expansion, program changes, and new technologies—as the City's population increased to an estimated 66,000 residents in 2020.

- Provide a community-friendly facility with shared and multi-use meeting spaces that could be used by neighborhood groups.

- Have a building design, in harmony with the surrounding community, that also served as an attractive catalyst for the development of high-end office and mixed-use buildings in the surrounding blocks.

- Be an attractive and efficient work environment with natural light, amenities, and optimum space adjacencies.

- Allow separation of visitor, staff, and prisoner traffic in both exterior and interior circulation.

- Incorporate building and security features that would withstand both human and natural threats.

- Include materials and systems that could withstand heavy use 24 hours a day, 7 days a week.

- Incorporate systems and spaces that could be quickly converted to emergency operations uses.

- Have standard police station features, including a holding area, shooting range, and bulletproof exterior walls.

The City also mandated that the police station be a green building that would earn LEED certification and act as a catalyst for future sustainable building design and construction in Woodland.

The City of Woodland wanted all of this on a $200 per-square-foot budget, the standard budget for a traditionally designed police facility in California.

So, LPA designed a 52,300-square-foot police station for the centrally located 3.2-acre site using efficiency and sustainability as the driving design elements of the project. A 7,100-square-foot Community Plaza provides a grand entry to the facility. The police station has a two-story, 42,845-square-foot main building with a public side, including the lobby and a community room, and a secured side for the various police functions.

A single-story 10,745-square-foot service building houses the SWAT/CNT, Motorbike Patrol, Bike Patrol, K-9 Patrol, and a state-of-the-art basement shooting range. LPA also created a public parking lot, a secured police parking lot, and room for future expansion.

And LPA did much more.

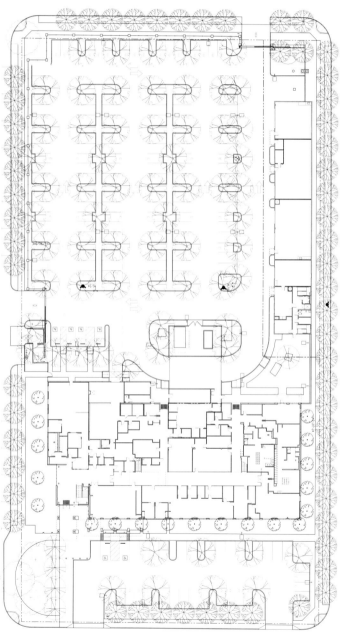

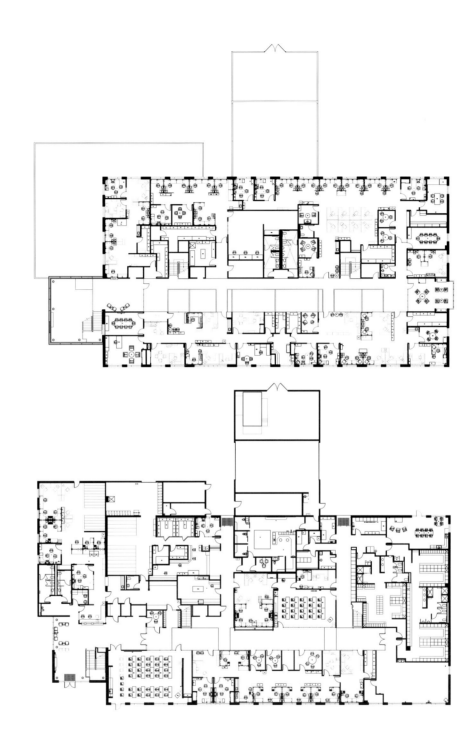

A green police station

To turn the police station green, LPA gave it an east–west orientation to reduce the buildings' solar heat gain. Windows on the south side of the buildings are smaller and have shading devices that keep out the hot sunlight in the summer and allow sun penetration into the buildings in the winter when heat is needed. The main building's daylight monitor—basically, a long, solar-oriented skylight—is oriented to the north to provide solar control and evenly distributed interior daylighting.

The 10-inch-thick concrete tilt-up wall panels provide a high degree of insulation and also a secure, blast- and bullet-resistant perimeter. A "cool roof" reflects sunlight and reduces heat gain. Reflective, Low-E window glazing also helps reduce heat gain within the buildings. Exterior lighting, including cutoff luminaries, is designed to reduce light trespass onto adjacent properties and promote a dark sky.

Additional green exterior features include a future 70-kilowatt photovoltaic panel system mounted on the south-facing roof elevation and recycled materials in the concrete paving, slabs, and tilt-up wall panels. Metal canopies at the lobby and south-facing windows shield pedestrians from the sun and rain.

The station has 9 on-street visitor parking spaces, a 33-space visitor parking lot, and a 117-space secured parking area with two gated entries for police vehicles. LPA landscaped the parking lots with an array of shade trees to reduce the heat island effect. An extensive bioswale system—open channels planted with grasses and other vegetation—filters stormwater from the parking lots and on the site naturally.

The major green interior feature of the main building is a two-story glass-walled central atrium running the length of the east side of the building. With the help of the daylight monitor and an interior translucent glass system, the atrium pours natural light into the building core and interior office spaces. In fact, 90 percent of the interior receives natural daylight, and 75 percent of the regularly occupied spaces have views to the outside.

By bringing natural daylight into the building core, the atrium reduces the use of electricity and artificial lighting. Sensors monitor the amount of daylight reaching the interior and adjust the indirect lighting system—which is more efficient and effective at distributing light than typical recessed parabolic lighting—accordingly. The atrium also exhausts hot air through louvers along the daylight monitor.

The station's faucets, shower heads, and toilets were designed to reduce water usage by 30 percent more than the current plumbing code requires. This project recycled 94 percent of its construction waste.

The police station exceeds California's Title 24 energy code requirements by 23.6 percent.

Insulation is provided by the 10-inch-thick concrete tilt-up walls. Both the main and service buildings have a standard four-pipe fan coil HVAC system with high efficiency motors that is more than 10 percent more efficient than that required by California's Title 24. A roof-mounted intake fan with a humidifier provides outside air ventilation to the majority of the main building. The basement shooting range in the service building is ventilated with 100 percent outside air and cooled with an evaporative air unit. A diesel-driven generator will provide emergency power back-up to critical building systems.

Assuring high indoor air quality was a major consideration. The main building underwent a two-week flush-out process when construction was completed that exhausted all fumes from the interior features, like furniture and computer equipment. Then, new filters were installed in the fan units to remove any of the captured contaminants. Indoor building materials, furniture, carpets, paints, and sealants were selected to meet LEED requirements for good indoor air quality. Copy machine areas have direct vent systems that exhaust hazardous fumes. All HVAC units, refrigerators, and drinking fountains use ozone-safe chemicals. Built-in walk-off mats at the building entrances collect possible contaminants that might be carried on footwear.

Safety, connection, and flexibility

LPA designed the overall physical layout of the police station for the physical safety of those who work there without suggesting that the City is, in any way, overly concerned with security. The arrangement of the entrances and circulation areas, for example, controls public access to all parts of the station. Public access spaces are also completely separated from secured areas of the station.

The interior of the main building is divided into a public west side and a secured east side. All the various police functions, including records, evidence storage, sallyport (a highly secured garage where detainees are physically transferred from police vehicles to the holding area inside the main building), and the holding area are located on the secured side of the main building.

The first floor of the main building has a sunlit two-story public lobby with a grand staircase, perimeter clerestory windows, a public mural space, and counter access to the Records, Traffic, and Investigation departments. A community room adjacent to the lobby doubles as a meeting space for both the public and the police, and it can be transformed into an emergency operations room.

The Records, Evidence, and Patrol departments are organized on the first floor to provide easy access to the public and secured parking areas. The Patrol department's holding area, for example, has direct access from the secured lot and through its sallyport. A 12-foot-wide first-floor corridor provides generous circulation space that encourages informal staff interactions.

The second-floor departments are organized around the 18-foot-wide atrium. Bridges and balconies cross the atrium to connect the different departments and offices and encourage interaction.

The main building's open floor plans and 10-foot ceilings in all of the office areas give them the greatest amount of flexibility. Most of the departments also have extra space to support the growth in city employees from 101 to as many as 161 by the year 2020.

The service building is a utilitarian facility with space for SWAT and emergency vehicles, patrol motorcycles and bikes, the K-9 unit, a basement-level armory and shooting range, and a large evidence storage room. Skylights bring natural daylight into the motorcycle and bicycle work room, storage, and circulation areas.

Construction of Woodland's green police station began in September 2002, and was completed in February 2004.

Project: City of Woodland Police Station
Location: Woodland, California
Size: 52,300 square feet
Construction cost: $11 million

Green features:

- East–west orientation reduces solar heat gain.
- Windows on the south side of the buildings have shading devices.
- Reflective, Low-E window glazing.
- The main building's daylight monitor is oriented to the north to provide solar control and evenly distributed interior daylighting.
- Two-story glass-walled central atrium brings consistent natural light into the interior.
- 90 percent of the interior receives natural daylight, and 75 percent of the regularly occupied spaces have views to the outside.
- Indirect lighting system automatically dims according to amount of natural light.
- A "cool roof" reflects sunlight and reduces heat gain.
- Exceeds California's Title 24 energy code requirements by 23.6 percent.
- Copy machine areas have direct vent systems that exhaust hazardous fumes.
- All HVAC units, refrigerators, and drinking fountains use ozone-safe chemicals.
- Exterior lighting reduces light trespass onto adjacent properties and promotes a dark sky.
- Water usage reduced by 30 percent.
- Recycled materials in the concrete paving, slabs, and tilt-up wall panels.
- Parking lots landscaped with shade trees to reduce the heat island effect.
- Extensive bioswale system filters stormwater.
- 94 percent of construction waste was recycled.

CHAPTER 7

Sonoma State University, which opened its Rohnert Park, California campus in 1961, embarked on a sustainability program in 1998 and completed four projects. By 2002, Sonoma State's campus and student population had grown large enough to support a new Student Recreation Center. The University decided that the new Center would be the first Sonoma State building to be designed according to the U.S. Green Building Council's rigorous LEED criteria.

The University engaged LPA to design the Student Recreation Center and to provide construction administration. The two-story, 53,000-square-foot center was completed in July 2004.

Fixing the mistakes of the past

The 269-acre Sonoma State University is located at the eastern edge of suburban Rohnert Park, California in the Sonoma County wine country, an hour's drive north of San Francisco. It is bordered by residential suburbs to the south and west, and by the primarily undeveloped green-clad Sonoma Mountains to the north and east, providing a dramatic natural backdrop for the campus.

Unfortunately, the school's 1960s buildings were designed as statements of the moment or as statements of style, not as a reflection of their location and function. They have, for example, small windows that don't open, that don't bring in sufficient natural light, and that don't provide views of the beautiful surrounding environment.

These buildings created a could-be-anywhere college campus. As they neared the end of their useful lives at the turn of the century, the University took that opportunity to begin replacing

SONOMA STATE UNIVERSITY STUDENT RECREATION CENTER
ROHNERT PARK, CALIFORNIA

them with new buildings that reflect the region's topography, landscape, and culture and that create a memorable identity and sense of place.

The University had even more objectives for its new Student Recreation Center. It wanted:

- A building that would manifest the new campus aesthetic.

- A building that would serve as a major gateway to the campus.

- A state-of-the-art Recreation Center that would also be a comfortable community center for all students.

- A building that would begin "re-imaging" the campus through its location and design, and by using natural building materials that better reflect the rural central Sonoma County environment.

- To demonstrate its commitment to sustainable design by adhering to the LEED Silver criteria in the design and construction of the Recreation Center.

- A building whose design and construction would educate users and passersby about the environment and sustainability.

The University wanted to do all of this on a typical California university state budget for a building of this type.

A contextual design for the present and future

To act as a major gateway to the campus, the Recreation Center was located adjacent to the University's primary pedestrian pathway. It opens onto the central quadrangle. The University Center, a planned future building to the south (also designed by LPA), will share the campus' entry courtyard with the Recreation Center.

The Recreation Center has a 2,000-square-foot main lobby with a central gallery that connects all of the spaces. To the east of the lobby is a 35-foot-tall rock climbing tower that serves as a landmark public space on the campus. The building also has a 5,500-square-foot single court gymnasium and indoor soccer arena to the west of the lobby, an 11,000-square-foot two-court gymnasium with an elevated running track on the northwest side of the Center, two multipurpose studios, fitness rooms, lockers, offices, and support spaces.

The Recreation Center utilizes a spread footing foundation system with load bearing concrete masonry unit walls, a concrete and metal deck floor and roof structure, and roof trusses.

Wood trellises shade the built-in seating that extends along the south façade across from the central quadrangle, encouraging students to stop and interact. The canopies on the southern façade create patterns of shade and shadow against the glass lobby façade and solid gym walls, minimizing solar gain and helping to break up the large building masses.

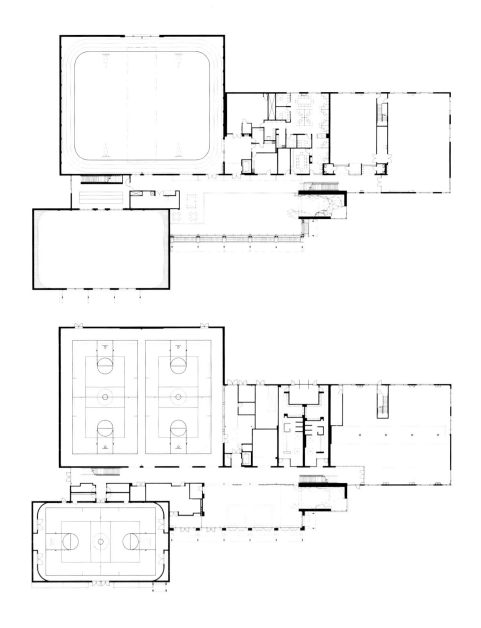

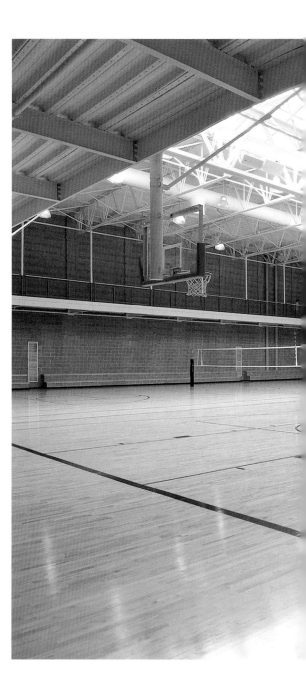

The Recreation Center's palette of natural and contextual building materials—Alaskan yellow cedar, stone, glass, and a standing seam metal roof—replicates materials used elsewhere on the campus, and complements the University's natural setting. The sunlit two-story lobby, which was designed as an extension of the central quadrangle, has a tongue-and-groove certified cedar ceiling and exposed Alaskan cedar Glu-Lam (a glue-laminated engineered structural wood product) beams, a natural slate floor, and a check-in desk using recycled materials.

LPA's interior design theme for the Center also focused on an indoor environment that reflected the lively physical activities of its users. The exposed interior building structure of Glu-Lam beams maximized ceiling heights, while the use of sunlight and natural building materials created a warm, welcoming space for all students.

A green Recreation Center

LPA designed Sonoma State University's new Student Recreation Center to meet LEED's Silver criteria, although the University has chosen to avoid the cost of applying for certification.

The Center is oriented on a north–south axis that promotes natural daylighting and solar control. Approximately 85 percent of the building's interior receives natural light from the lobby's and gallery's southern glass façade, operable windows, clerestories, and from translucent glass skylights, including an 80-foot-long skylight over the center of the main gymnasium. The exterior windows are insulated and have Low-E glazing that brings sunlight without heat into the building's interior. A state-of-the-art lighting control system monitors the amount of daylight in the interior and adjusts the artificial lighting system accordingly.

Nearly 70 percent of the Student Recreation Center is naturally ventilated and cooled through vented skylights, operable windows, vents in the façade's built-in seating, and a night flush of all hot air, which helps to moderate the building's temperature. An indirect evaporative cooling system and a radiant heat floor system serve the lobby and fitness rooms. The small gymnasium has a destratification ventilation system that brings in air low to the floor. The warming air rises and displaces through the space without mechanical ventilation.

The building's design uses wooden trellises as solar shading devices on the south façade, which lets natural daylight into the interior of the building while minimizing solar heat gain, which reduces air conditioning demands and energy costs.

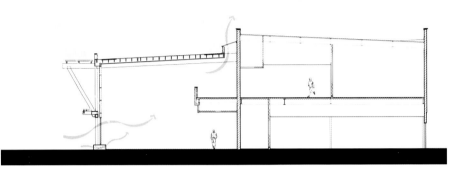

The Student Recreation Center is 50 percent more efficient than required by California's Title 24 energy code.

Green building materials used throughout the Student Recreation Center include recycled content carpeting, natural linoleum made from jute and linseed oil, recycled glass tiles, wood from FSC (Forest Stewardship Council) certified forests, and recycled materials for the solid surface counters. All of the furniture also has a high recycled content.

A signature building

The signature element of the Recreation Center is the 35-foot-tall glass and rock climbing tower, which provides exercise for students and—thanks to views through the southern glass façade—terrific entertainment for passersby and people using the student quadrangle. At night, the illuminated tower becomes a lantern for the University and its students.

The Student Recreation Center broke ground in January 2003. Two existing buildings on the site were demolished and 75 percent of the materials were recycled. In addition, 90 percent of the construction waste was recycled. Construction of the Center was completed in July 2004.

Project: Sonoma State University Student
Recreation Center
Location: Rohnert Park, California
Size: 53,000 square feet
Construction cost: $11 million
Green features:
· North-south orientation promotes natural daylighting and solar control.
· Approximately 85 percent of the interior receives natural light.
· Exterior windows are insulated and have Low-E glazing.
· State-of-the-art lighting control system.
· Nearly 70 percent of the Student Recreation Center is naturally ventilated and cooled.
· The small gymnasium has a destratification ventilation system.
· Wooden trellises act as solar shading devices on the south façade.
· The Center is 50 percent more efficient than required by California's Title 24 energy code.
· Recycled and natural building and finish materials.
· All of the furniture has a high recycled content.

CHAPTER 8

The low-rise 75,000-square-foot Cesar Chavez Elementary School—a kindergarten through fifth-grade school for 800 children completed in downtown Long Beach, California in September 2004—was one of the first true green K–12 schools in California, a significant accomplishment for anyone who cares about our children and our educators.

Demonstrated benefits of green schools

Green schools bring many benefits to our children and communities. First, green schools are healthier places to learn and work. They bring abundant natural daylight and fresh air into the classrooms and other indoor facilities. Green schools also use building materials—from wall paint to composite wood products—that do not "off-gas" the toxic volatile organic compounds (VOCs) often found in standard materials. Natural linoleum made from linseed oil and jute rather than the VOC-laden vinyl composition tile, for example, is attractive, durable, and highly recyclable at the end of its useful life.

Second, green schools demonstrably improve learning. A 1999 study by the Heschong Mahone Group of the Fort Collins, Colorado, Orange County, California, and Seattle, Washington school districts found that students in classrooms with the most daylighting progressed 20 percent faster on math tests and 26 percent faster on reading tests than students in classrooms with the least daylighting.

Third, green schools have minimal negative impact on the environment, particularly compared to standard schools. Sustainable site planning, for example, minimizes grading, which reduces the likelihood of erosion.

Cesar Chavez
Elementary School
Long Beach,
California

Fourth, green schools significantly reduce those all-important overhead costs, enabling school districts to put school funds back where they belong: in the classroom.

Fifth, schools don't have to be new to be green. Existing, standard-construction schools—which outnumber planned new schools by four to one—can undergo a green renovation, spreading healthier and more efficient educational facilities to every corner of our communities.

Thurston Middle School in Laguna Beach, California, for example, underwent an LPA-designed green renovation. New windows and skylights in all exterior-facing classrooms now bring natural light into the school. Motion sensors adjust artificial lighting in a room according to sunlight and activity, reducing energy consumption. A room-length skylight floods the library with natural sunlight, minimizing the need for artificial illumination. Thurston Middle School also received a State of California grant covering installation of a rooftop photovoltaic system that will provide 8 percent of the school's energy needs.

Finally, a green school is a genuine "living laboratory" where students and educators expand their environmental understanding and conservation activities far beyond contributing to classroom recycling bins. The schools themselves are educational tools.

Of course, many people assume that green schools cost too much money, that green is a high-priced luxury that hard-pressed school districts cannot afford. The truth, however, is that the price of green building materials, mechanical systems, and furniture is now comparable to that of their standard counterparts.

A variety of State and Federal incentive programs, and even public utility programs, also help to fund green construction and renovation, further reducing their cost.

Cesar Chavez Elementary School, completed within the parameters of the State of California's school allocation budget, is proof of this, and it has shown all school districts how they, too, can turn their schools green on standard budgets. It even won design awards from the Orange County and Long Beach AIA chapters, proving that building green doesn't mean a facility can't also be beautiful.

Much more than green
The 2.6-acre Cesar Chavez Elementary School site was two blocks east of the Los Angeles River and three blocks north of the Pacific Ocean in downtown Long Beach, California. The site lay between the newer and more affluent World Trade Center downtown business district and an older, moderate income residential neighborhood that had been on a downward spiral prior to the City's redevelopment efforts. The western side of the school was adjacent to Cesar E. Chavez Park, a then-new 7-acre neighborhood park that was furthering the renaissance of the adjacent residential neighborhood.

This location was critical to the City of Long Beach and the Long Beach Unified School District. In addition to using Cesar Chavez Elementary to showcase intelligent, environmentally responsible, sustainable building design for a municipal school, the aim was to:

- Strengthen this rapidly improving section of downtown Long Beach by uniting two disparate adjacent districts and creating a more pedestrian-friendly public realm.

- Create a technologically advanced elementary school.

- Change the existing institutional nature of recent city school projects into a welcoming environment for 800 children.

In response, LPA designed a green school with 34 classrooms, including a special-education classroom, a gymnasium that also serves as a multipurpose room for the community after-hours and on weekends, administration offices, a library, a computer learning center, and a separate kindergarten playground. A covered lunch shelter provides both protection from the elements and abundant natural light. A portion of the adjacent Cesar E. Chavez Park is closed off for student activities during the school day.

Technology infrastructure throughout the campus includes the computer lab adjacent to the library, a main signal room in the gymnasium, and 34 teaching stations with 6 to 8 computer stations each. A series of shared work rooms between each cluster of classrooms has additional data connections.

Green features

Several green strategies shaped LPA's functional and aesthetic design of the school. Aside from the central plant, which the School District requested, none of the green features cost any more than standard components, and all of them help to reduce the school's annual operating costs.

- The school was carefully sited on the 2.6-acre property to give it an east–west orientation that reaps the greatest benefits from the sun and wind. The main façades face north and south. The north façade has many large windows that bring natural daylight into the school, while the south façade has a variety of shading features to keep out sun heat and glare. The east–west orientation also enhances the school's natural ventilation system.

- Classrooms, the gymnasium, offices, and public spaces are filled with abundant natural light. Operable northern windows with low emission (Low-E) laminated glazing in the classrooms and public areas bring in daylight. Natural daylighting is also filtered through a series of lightshelves and sunscreens, as well as light monitors in the roof, which bring northern light into the public areas, including the corridors. (Windows on the east and west exposures were kept to a minimum and sunshades were used when necessary.) The lunch shelter has a series of linear saw-toothed skylights that bring in natural light.

- Horizontal sunscreens, canopies, and shading on the southern façade provide optimum light control. A dimming system in the classrooms, offices, and public areas automatically lowers or shuts down the indirect and direct T8 fluorescent lighting when sufficient daylighting is present, which saves electricity. This was the first use of indirect school lighting in the Long Beach Unified School District's history.

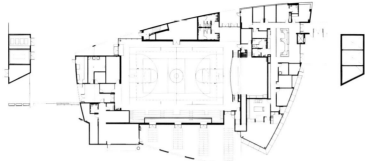

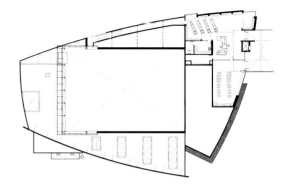

Occupancy sensors shut off lighting when no one is present in a room, further saving electricity.

· Low-E glass in all the windows stops the direct transmission of heat, but not sunlight. Low-E glass can reduce heat transmission by as much as 70 percent. Awnings, sunscreens, and shades along the south façade also block solar heat gain and lower HVAC costs.

· LPA also oriented the school to support natural ventilation, created by a series of operable clerestories and windows that provide great cross-ventilation and cool the classrooms. This was the first use of a natural ventilation system in the school district. Operable skylights vent air from the common areas. Light monitors in the roof also conduct heat out of the school. This system significantly reduces HVAC needs and costs.

· The roof has R-30 insulation.

· A central water-cooled HVAC plant with four-pipe fan coil units provides greater efficiency, lower costs, and ease of maintenance compared to a package unit system. While initially more expensive than a package unit system, the plant provides long-term cost savings through lower energy and maintenance costs.

· Together, these lighting and environmental control systems reduce energy usage and costs by 33 percent more than is required by the California Title 24 energy code.

· The school was constructed with natural, recycled, and recyclable building materials. Many floors, for example, are covered in natural linoleum made from linseed oil and jute, rather than the standard vinyl composition tile (VCT). (The linoleum is also highly recyclable at the end of its useful life.) Carpets and wall coverings have a significant amount of recycled content. The kindergarten play area's rubber surface was manufactured from several recycled rubber sources. Aluminum edging manufactured with recycled content was used instead of steel or concrete to separate the landscape areas.

· Recycling bins in each classroom collect paper, plastic, and aluminum.

· Rather than heat-absorbing AC paving, concrete was used for the school's main drive aisle and on the hard courts. The higher reflective value of the concrete helps to reduce heat gain by as much as 50 percent.

- Trees planted between the parking court and the northern side of the school, and trees planted around the perimeter and along the bordering streets, help to shade the campus and reduce the number and intensity of heat islands. The trees also beautify the campus and present an attractive and welcoming public realm to the adjacent residential neighborhood and business district, rather than an asphalt sea of parking lots.

- A green screen planted with blood red trumpet vine along the south-facing wall of the lunch shelter that stretches toward the park shades the gymnasium/administration building and provides a 20-foot-long landscaping element, the school's major landscape feature, that is safe from foot traffic and potential damage.

- The irrigation system—low precipitation rate spray heads and bubblers, and an evapotranspiration-based water management system—reduces runoff and landscape and domestic water usage by as much as 30 percent or more.

- Prior to the school's opening, 1,800 neighborhood children were bussed daily to area schools. Now, 800 students are no longer bussed to other schools. Indeed, many children now walk or ride their bicycles to Cesar Chavez Elementary School, which saves fuel and reduces air pollution generated by the School District's diesel-powered school buses.

A living laboratory

At Long Beach Unified School District and community meetings about the design for Cesar Chavez Elementary School, LPA introduced the green school concept and quickly garnered enthusiastic support for the cost-effective green features that would create a healthy and attractive environment for 800 children during the school day, and for the community users during off-school hours.

The students are learning about and experiencing the natural environment on a daily, practical basis by studying in natural daylight rather than under artificial lighting, breathing in fresh air rather than recycled air, walking to and from school on tree-shaded sidewalks, and contributing to the recycling bins in their classrooms.

The surrounding community is learning about the power of the natural environment as they see the almost daily changes made to their neighborhoods and their lives by the enhanced public realm and a school facility that has raised the bar for the entire area. The Long Beach Unified School District is learning the many benefits of green design for students, teachers, and administrators, and it is seeing the lower energy, water consumption, and costs generated by that green design.

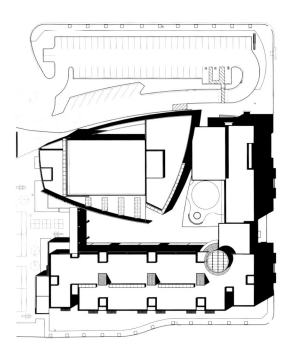

Multipurpose architectural design

LPA created an architectural design for the three two-story main buildings that reflects, symbolizes, and unites the disparate adjoining districts. The buildings' burnished concrete block base is nearly maintenance-free and vandal-resistant.

Building #1: Gymnasium/multipurpose room, library, computer learning center, and administration offices along West Third Street. This building—which borders the Cesar E. Chavez Park on the west and the redeveloping residential district of existing Craftsman and Spanish bungalows, Art Deco apartment buildings, and new market rate housing on the north—has an edge of sweeping, angular rooflines, curving dark taupe plaster, and burnished concrete block walls that reach out to Cesar E. Chavez Park.

Building #2: Classroom block along Maine Avenue. The linear, horizontal, staggered architecture of dark taupe plaster and burnished concrete block walls gives this building, which borders the World Trade Center downtown business district, an urban edge. The main circulation stair and elevator are found in a truncated cone clad in reddish brown metal panels.

Building #3: Classroom block along West Broadway. Like Building #2, linear, horizontal, staggered architecture gives this building, which also borders the World Trade Center downtown business district, an urban edge. Sunshade awnings protect the south-facing windows.

Lunch shelter: This structure defines the northern side of the central quad. The skylit ceiling provides abundant natural light, and the exterior green screen creates a wall of landscape through the campus.

Central quad: The space where the four Cesar Chavez Elementary School buildings meet forms the inner central quad. This design provides sufficient security, so the school does not have to be wrapped with ugly and isolating security fencing. A large specimen tree provides shade. Beds of durable indigenous plants define the tricycle path within the kindergarten play area. The horizontal green screen defines the lunch shelter. This landscape is both low maintenance and durable.

Kindergarten play area: This play area is adjacent to the Maine Avenue classroom block and provides the centerpiece for the campus quad. A tricycle path winds through the circular space. The durable and safe rubber surfacing protects children using the colorful climbing equipment. A golden rain tree is wrapped by built-in benches, giving children a shaded place to sit and relax.

Main play area: Located on the west side of the campus, the main play area is a joint-use component within Cesar E. Chavez Park. The grass area has not been defined with specific activities, allowing the students to determine what the area will become. The hardscape area has basketball courts, ball walls, hopscotch, and tether ball.

A welcoming interior design

The school interior continues the exterior design aesthetic with its colors, materials, and forms. LPA used light woods extensively throughout the interior. Organic accent colors like deep burnt orange and sage green help to define the quad areas and animate the interior corridors.

Classrooms: The colors were kept light and bright—soft gray-blues, muted greens, and reds. Operable windows allow the ocean breezes to sweep through the classrooms. "Teaching walls" have sliding white boards (not dusty chalkboards) and integrated storage units.

Gymnasium/multipurpose room: Laminated glass windows with a translucent inner layer protect this room from glare, direct sunlight, and heat gain, while bringing in an abundance of natural light. A stage doubles as an additional teaching station.

Computer learning center: This center is large enough to accommodate a standard classroom of students and has a separate exterior entry to encourage use.

Library: The library was designed to make an architectural and welcoming statement as part of the school's front entrance. The interior design integrates the materials and colors used throughout the campus with varied ceiling heights and distinctive lighting systems. Two large north-facing windows define the main stack space and a corner reading room, which is perched over the administration offices.

Administration offices: LPA designed these offices to define the front door to the campus. Steel pivoting gates provide a secure off-hour entry into the central quad. Lighting, materials, and an abundance of natural daylight provide a light, bright, and welcoming environment for students and visitors.

Multipurpose landscape architecture

LPA designed the landscape architecture to serve both the school and the surrounding community, and to forge stronger ties between the disparate adjacent uses.

LPA used trees throughout the campus to reduce heat islands, shade children and adults, help beautify the school, and enhance the public realm. The parking court on the north side of the site is separated from the school buildings by a large continuous planter holding canopy trees to shade the parking lot. The planter gives the shade trees greater room for root growth so they can grow taller and shade a greater portion of the hardscape than standard tree cutouts would have allowed. As the school's northern façade has many large windows, students look out not onto a sea of asphalt but onto beautiful shade trees.

Trees planted along the perimeter of the campus and along the street further help to shade the parking area, as well as portions of the sidewalks and streets. As a result, the adjacent residential neighborhood and business district look out upon beautiful shade trees and other landscaping elements.

Trees were also planted along the south, west, and east facades of the school buildings—which have the greatest amount of sun exposure—to provide natural shading and filtered light.

The lunch shelter's 20-foot-long curved south-facing wall, lined with a green screen planted with blood red trumpet vine, adds a continuous landscape element to the school, and it reaches west into the 7-acre Cesar E. Chavez Park, drawing the park landscape into the inner campus.

97

The irrigation system uses highly efficient low precipitation rate spray heads and bubblers, as well as an evapotranspiration-based water management system that includes a rain sensor and a flow sensor that can shut off all or part of the system in the event of rain or a line break. These water conservation systems help to reduce the school's runoff and irrigation and domestic water use by at least 30 percent.

Project: Cesar Chavez Elementary School
Location: Downtown Long Beach, California
Size: 75,000 square feet
Construction cost: $17 million
Green features:
· East–west orientation reaps the greatest benefits from the sun and wind.
· Natural ventilation system via operable clerestories, windows, and skylights.
· Abundant natural daylight from large operable north-facing windows, lightshelves, sunscreens, skylights, and rooftop light monitors.
· Low-E laminated window glazing and a variety of shading features to keep out sun heat and glare.
· Automatic system lowers or shuts down the indirect and direct T8 fluorescent lighting when sufficient daylighting is present.
· A central water-cooled HVAC plant with four-pipe fan coil units. Operable skylights vent air from the common areas. Light monitors in the roof also conduct heat out of the school.
· Energy usage and costs are reduced by 33 percent more than required by the California Title 24 energy code.
· Natural, recycled, and recyclable building materials.
· Landscaping, including abundant trees, reduces the number and intensity of heat islands. A green screen shades the gymnasium/administration building.
· Landscape and domestic water usage is reduced by at least 30 percent.

Financing a green school

Some of the costs of the $15-million project were offset by two different programs:

- Savings By Design: Cesar Chavez Elementary was the first LPA-designed K–12 school to participate in Savings By Design, a program sponsored by four of California's largest utilities under the auspices of the Public Utilities Commission. Savings By Design encourages high performance non-residential building design and construction by providing a range of services, including owner incentives to help offset the costs of energy efficient building features.

- Proposition 47. Cesar Chavez Elementary was the first school to make use of the Proposition 47 Energy Allowance Grant, a State school facility grant program that helped fund the school's design and construction.

In addition, because Cesar Chavez Elementary is a joint-use facility shared with the city's Parks and Recreation Department—which uses the gymnasium building and other recreational facilities during off-school hours—the Department provided additional funding to construct the school.

Cesar Chavez Elementary School broke ground in Spring 2003. It was completed in September 2004, and opened for its first students on September 18–19, 2004, setting the benchmark for green schools, even green school districts, everywhere.

Our children and educators spend six to eight hours or more a day, five days a week, in school buildings. Their health, psychological well being, and stress levels are all directly affected by those buildings. Clearly, green schools are necessary not only for our children and educators, but also for our communities and the planet.

What are we waiting for?

CHAPTER 9

LPA doesn't just talk about green buildings. We actively practice what we preach.

In January 2004, LPA completed the green retrofit of 28,000 square feet of ground floor office space for its new headquarters in a several-year-old office/R&D building at the University Research Park in Irvine, California.

The project was part of the U.S. Green Building Council's LEED-CI pilot program—which promotes high performance, healthy, durable, and environmentally sound workplaces—and in cooperation with the University of California at Irvine (UCI) and The Irvine Company.

On a Tenant Improvement allowance of just $30 per square foot—the typical allowance given by suburban California landlords—LPA turned its new headquarters into a real-world model of sustainable workplace development that earned LEED certification. This project—more than any highly publicized, high cost showplace—truly demonstrates what is possible in green commercial renovations.

LPA's model—which can be replicated in most Tenant Improvement projects across the country— can create a healthier and more productive work environment for employees that helps attract and retain skilled workers, and it can save a company money through reduced energy, HVAC, lighting, and water costs, all on a cost-effective TI allowance.

PRACTICING WHAT WE PREACH— LPA, INC.'S GREEN OFFICE
IRVINE, CALIFORNIA

A sustainable design lab

LPA turned that ubiquitous American real estate product—the low-rise suburban office park building—into a model sustainable workplace. This $300-million, 185-acre business campus for high-tech, R&D, professional offices, light manufacturing, and corporate business headquarters is being developed by The Irvine Company on land adjacent to, and leased from UCI. LPA designed the low-rise campus buildings. The park's first phase opened in 1996.

In May 2000, University Research Park was designated by the Department of Energy as a "Power Park," a living laboratory for the demonstration and evaluation of advanced power and energy technologies and management systems. URP's two-story buildings were enhanced with new infrastructure, including augmented natural gas lines and extra communication conduits, to help support future energy and sustainable technologies.

Prior to 2004, LPA's 175 Irvine, California employees worked in two separate buildings. LPA wanted to create greater efficiency and enhance its creative and collaborative process by consolidating those employees into one facility. LPA had worked with both The Irvine Company and UCI's APEP (Advanced Power and Energy Program) department on several projects in the past. Knowing of the research relationships available at URP, the firm approached the two joint venture partners about leasing space at URP and turning its long-standing expertise in sustainable design and its need for a new headquarters facility into a Sustainable Design Lab project that would research, implement, and test sustainable practices and new technologies.

The firm chose a 62,000-square-foot, two-story, flexible and contemporary-style tilt-up office building that was originally constructed in 2001. The building's north–south orientation, efficient building footprint, large and plentiful windows, abundant natural light, large open space interior, and native landscaping made the structure the ideal choice for LPA's Sustainable Design Lab project.

LPA's primary objective was to create a model of cost-effective sustainable interior design and technologies for existing office buildings. The design would have to be flexible to enable the building to respond to and test new technologies and sustainable programs in the future. The firm also wanted to demonstrate that sustainable design is not limited by budget, programming, or architecture, and that building green can benefit any new construction or renovation project. Finally, LPA wanted a model that would give the firm's designers accurate data about the effectiveness of a wide variety of sustainable strategies that will help guide its work on current and future client projects.

LPA began renovating its URP office in October 2003. The firm moved into its new headquarters on January 2, 2004.

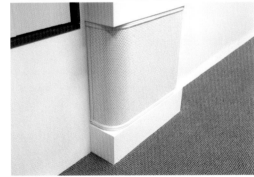

A sustainable workplace

LPA's new headquarters is part of the U.S. Green Building Council's LEED Commercial Interior pilot program. The office is one of the first occupied spaces in the country using these new criteria for interiors and received LEED-CI certification in 2005.

LPA drew on its in-house architecture, interior design, graphics, and furniture design resources to maximize its budget and create an attractive, functional, and green work space. This integration of services—team members working together to meet the larger project objectives of a functional green building—is a sustainable design strategy that makes green elements part of a building's DNA.

Through this process, LPA incorporated a wide variety of sustainable technologies, features, and practices into its new headquarters, including:

HVAC: The headquarters is served by an energy efficient variable frequency drive system that was retrofitted into the existing air handler by The Irvine Company as part of its URP-wide energy efficiency program.

Lighting: By eliminating private offices and moving all fixed walls to the interior of the space, the design allows 100 percent of the firm's employees to enjoy natural daylighting. A state-of-the-art system automatically turns artificial lights on and off depending on the level of natural daylighting and the activity or inactivity of people in the space.

Energy: The highly efficient HVAC, lighting, and electrical systems used throughout LPA's new headquarters contribute to an environment that exceeds California's Title 24 energy standards by 22 percent.

103

Indoor air quality: LPA's indoor air quality construction plan included strategies like coordinating the construction sequencing of wet and dry activities to avoid contaminating dry materials that would absorb moisture and become a breeding ground for mold or bacteria growth. Low VOC (Volatile Organic Compounds) materials were used throughout the interior, including paints, sealants, adhesives, carpet tiles, and linoleum made with linseed oil. None of the equipment LPA provided—including air conditioning equipment for the computer servers—use CFC-based refrigerants. The headquarters also has a carbon dioxide monitoring system. Together, these strategies, products, and tools have created a healthy indoor environment.

Water: By switching to waterless urinals and low-flow fixtures in the restrooms, the headquarters' water usage has been reduced by 21 percent compared to similar speculative development projects in the region.

Recycled materials: LPA used recycled materials throughout the headquarters. The main conference room carpet, for example, is made from 100 percent recycled materials. Signage throughout the headquarters is 100 percent recycled plastic, and all the accent woods in the main entry doors, reception desk, and built-ins are Medium Density Fiberboard, a 100 percent recycled material.

Furniture system: The LPA-designed furniture system has a high percentage of recycled content. The divider panels and support brackets are 100 percent recycled steel. The desk/work surfaces are 100 percent recycled wood, and the filing cabinets are made with 40 percent recycled steel. Packaging and wrapping materials to ship the furniture were eliminated, reducing landfill waste.

As the furniture system components were manufactured within 55 miles of its headquarters, LPA significantly cut down on the pollution and costs of long-distance shipping, a major LEED consideration.

Recycled construction waste: More than half of all construction waste was recycled and diverted from landfills.

A design and technology showroom

The office interior was designed to demonstrate the headquarters' sustainable technologies and features for visitors and clients. The office was designed with a variety of ceiling treatments to show that LPA's sustainable model can work in any office building and with any interior design. A variety of carpets were used in the headquarters to demonstrate recycled—and recyclable—products that are available to LPA's clients.

A series of lobby graphics explain and document the sustainable features used in the headquarters. Graphics throughout the office also showcase the sustainable elements, educating and informing both employees and visitors that this headquarters has been designed differently for a purpose.

An LPA workplace

Even as a national model of sustainable design, this green headquarters ultimately must function as an attractive, efficient, and healthy workplace for LPA's employees.

The office has an 800-square-foot lobby, a 500-square-foot main conference room and several smaller conference rooms, a library, 180 collaborative workstations, and team work areas.

The headquarters floorplan is designed to maximize the collaborative process that is the focus of the firm's work. Areas for impromptu meetings off the major circulation spaces are linked to the more formal collaborative workstations, conference rooms, and group gathering spaces to promote a high degree of interaction.

By using a variety of ceiling designs and an open space layout, eliminating private offices, and locating fixed partitions only in the core of the building, 100 percent of the office interior receives abundant natural light. All work areas also have views to the outside.

LPA built flexibility into the open plan office design, so that it can easily and cost-effectively evolve as the firm, its staff, and its needs change through the years, and as LPA incorporates new sustainable technologies and strategies created in the future.

LPA, in partnership with Tangram Studio, designed the stylish, ergonomic furniture systems and cockpit-style workstations used throughout the office. The workstation design supports both left and right computer layouts. Users can lower or raise the horizontal platform—the desk/work surface—by up to 6 inches, according to their height, for greater comfort, efficiency, and sustained energy.

LPA has demonstrated at its renovated green headquarters that truly affordable green Tenant Improvement projects are not only possible, they're practical, and they can be done anywhere in the country.

Project: LPA's Green Office
Location: Irvine, California
Size: 28,000 square feet
Construction cost: $30 per square foot
                  Tenant Improvement
Green features:
· An energy efficient variable frequency drive HVAC system.
· 100 percent of the firm's employees enjoy natural daylighting.
· State-of-the-art system automatically turns artificial lights on and off.
· Exceeds California's Title 24 energy standards by 22 percent.
· Low-VOC materials used throughout the interior, including paints, sealants, adhesives, carpet tiles, and linoleum.
· No equipment uses CFC-based refrigerants.
· A carbon dioxide monitoring system.
· Waterless urinals and low-flow fixtures in the restrooms.
· Water usage reduced by 21 percent.
· Extensive use of recycled materials. The LPA-designed furniture system has a high percentage of recycled content.
· More than half of all construction waste was recycled.

MainstreamGreen

SustainableDesignByLPA FirmProfile

2005

American Society of Landscape Architects National
Honor Award: Toyota South Campus

American Institute of Architects California Council/"Savings by Design"
Merit Award: Cesar Chavez Elementary School

American Institute of Architects Orange County Chapter
Merit Award: Cesar Chavez Elementary School
Merit Award: The Press Enterprise Headquarters
Merit Award: Orange Coast College "ABC" Science Building
Merit Award: Mt. San Jacinto College, Menifee Campus, Technology Center

American Institute of Architects California Council/Concrete Masonry Association
Honor Award: Samueli Jewish Campus

American Institute of Architects California Council/Coalition for Adequate School Housing (C.A.S.H.)
Award of Excellence: Thurston Middle School
Award of Honor: Woodcrest Elementary School
Award of Honor: Cesar Chavez Elementary School

2004

American Institute of Architects Orange County Chapter
Honor Award: San Diego Jewish Academy
Honor Award: Tarbut V'Torah Upper School & Community Building at the Samueli Jewish Campus
Honorable Mention: Santiago Canyon College Science Building
Honorable Mention: Cuyamaca Community College Student Center
Honorable Mention: Shasta County Library

American Institute of Architects Central Valley Chapter
Merit Award: Woodland Police Facility Headquarters
Merit Award: Grayson Community Center

American Institute of Architects Redwood Empire
Citation: Sonoma State University Recreation Center

2003

American Institute of Architects California Council/"Savings by Design"
Merit Award: Premier Automotive Group, North American Headquarters

American Institute of Architects Orange County Chapter
Merit Award: Southwestern College LRC
Honorable Mention: Premier Automotive Group
Honorable Mention: Cypress College Maintenance Facility

American Institute of Architects Long Beach/South Bay Chapter
Honor Award Green Architecture: Toyota South Campus

2002

American Institute of Architects California Council
Merit Award: Mendez Intermediate School

American Institute of Architects Orange County Chapter
Honorable Mention: Halford Residence
Honorable Mention: Hector Godinez High School
Honorable Mention: Fire Station No. 51
Honorable Mention: Pacific Coast Campus LRC

**American Institute of Architects
California Council/Coalition for
Adequate School Housing (C.A.S.H.)**
Award of Excellence: Broadway/Golden
Elementary School
Award of Excellence: Hector Godinez High School
Award of Excellence: Escondido Elementary
Schools

2001

**American Institute of Architects
Orange County Chapter**
Honor Award: Mendez Intermediate School
Honorable Mention: Sage Hill School
Honorable Mention: Broadway/Golden
Elementary School

**American Institute of Architects
Long Beach/South Bay Chapter**
Honor Award: CSU Chancellor's Office
Honor Award: Broadway/Golden Elementary
School
Merit Award: Temple Willow Maintenance
Facility

2000

**American Institute of Architects
California Council/Concrete Masonry
Association**
Merit Award: Tarbut V'Torah Community Day
School

**American Institute of Architects
Orange County Chapter**
Merit Award: TGS Irvine Corporate Campus
Merit Award: Escondido Elementary Schools
Merit Award: Temple Willow Maintenance Facility

**American Institute of Architects
California Council/Coalition for
Adequate School Housing (C.A.S.H.)**
Honor Award: Running Springs Elementary
School

1999

**American Institute of Architects
Orange County Chapter**
Honor Award: Mission Imports
Honor Award: Mossimo Corporate Headquarters
Honorable Mention: CSU Chancellor's Office
Honorable Mention: Irvine Spectrum Fire Station
Honorable Mention: San Diego Jewish Academy

**American Institute of Architects
California Council/Coalition for
Adequate School Housing (C.A.S.H.)**
Award of Merit: Paramount Park K–8 School

1998

**American Institute of Architects
Orange County Chapter**
Honor Award: Tarbut V'Torah Community Day
School
Honorable Mention: Sage Hill School

1997

**American Institute of Architects
Orange County Chapter**
Merit Award: Mission Imports
Merit Award: Westwood Medical
Merit Award: Lake Hills Chapel

**American Society of Landscape Architects
Southern California Chapter**
Honor Award: South Chula Vista Library

**American Institute of Architects
Western Mountain Region**
Honor Award: Lake Hills Chapel

**American Institute of Architects
State of Colorado**
Honor Award: Lake Hills Chapel

**National American Institute of Architects
Religious Art & Architecture Awards**
National Award: Saddleback Valley Community
Church Interim Sanctuary

1996

**American Institute of Architects
Orange County Chapter**
Honor Award: Tarbut V'Torah Community Day
School
Merit Award: Saddleback Valley Community
Church Interim Sanctuary
Merit Award: Van Nuys Projects (Amtrak & DWP)
Merit Award: CSU Chancellor's Office
Honorable Mention: Anaheim Plaza
Honorable Mention: San Marcos City Hall

**American Institute of Architects
Orange County Urban Design Committee
Public Realm**
Merit Award: Tustin Marketplace
Merit Award: Anaheim Plaza

1995

**American Institute of Architects
Orange County Chapter**
Honor Award: Kubota Tractor
Merit Award: Spacesaver School
Honorable Mention: Lake Hills Chapel

**American Institute of Architects
San Diego Chapter**
Honor Award: South Chula Vista Library

Society of American Registered Architects
Award of Merit: CSU San Bernardino School of
Business

1994

**American Institute of Architects
Orange County Chapter**
Merit Award: Joint-Use Library, Rancho
Santiago College
Merit Award: Food 4 Less Retail Store

**American Institute of Architects
Central Valley Chapter**
Award: UC Davis Academic Surge Building

1993

**American Institute of Architects
Orange County Chapter**
Honor Award: Saddleback Valley Community
Church Interim Sanctuary
Honor Award: East Municipal Water District
Merit Award: El Camino Real Community Center

**American Institute of Architects
San Diego Chapter**
Citation of Recognition: Palomar College
Wellness Center

1992

American Institute of Architects
Orange County Chapter
Merit Award: Park Headquarters
Honorable Mention: Mission Viejo Town Center

American Institute of Architects
Central Valley Chapter
Merit Award: E. Coast National Scenic Area
Citation Award: Natomas Corporate Center

1991

American Institute of Architects
California Council
Honor Award: One Venture

American Institute of Architects
Orange County Chapter
Honor Award: Tustin Market Place
Merit Award: One Venture

1990

American Institute of Architects
California Council
Firm of the Year Award

American Institute of Architects
Orange County Chapter
Merit Award: Valley Telecommunications
Headquarters, DWP

American Institute of Architects
Cabrillo Chapter
Merit Award: Media City Center

1989

American Institute of Architects
California Council
Merit Award: River Center

American Institute of Architects
Orange County Chapter
Honor Award: University Montessori Preschool
Honor Award: CalMat Corporate Headquarters

1988

American Institute of Architects
Orange County Chapter
Honor Award: Galasso's Bakery
Honor Award: University Montessori Preschool

American Institute of Architects
Cabrillo Chapter
Merit Award: 100 Broadway Office

1987

American Institute of Architects
California Council
Honor Award: State Compensation Insurance
Fund Office
Merit Award: Renaissance Center Phase II

American Institute of Architects
Orange County Chapter
Honor Award: State Compensation Insurance
Fund Office
Merit Award: River Center Commercial Complex

1986

American Institute of Architects
Orange County Chapter

Honor Award: Calmat Corporate Headquarters

1985

American Institute of Architects
Orange County Chapter

Merit Award: Renaissance Center Phase II
Merit Award: Vintage Park Business Complex

1984

American Institute of Architects
California Council

Merit Award: Greystone Office Complex

American Institute of Architects
Orange County Chapter

Honorable Mention: Renaissance Center Phase II

1983

American Institute of Architects
Orange County Chapter

Merit Award: Subaru Distribution Center
Merit Award: Yuba City, City Hall
Honorable Mention: California Center

American Institute of Architects
The Masonry Institute

Honor Award: Yuba City, City Hall

1982

American Institute of Architects
Orange County Chapter

Merit Award: North Ranch Office Development

American Institute of Architects
South Bay Chapter

Commendation: Mission Park

1981

American Institute of Architects
Orange County Chapter

Honorable Mention: Greystone Office Complex
Honorable Mention: Larkspur Landing Retail

1979

American Institute of Architects
Orange County Chapter

Merit Award: Harold Hutton Sports Center

1977

American Institute of Architects
Orange County Chapter

Honorable Mention: Willows Retail

1971

American Institute of Architects
Orange County Chapter

Citation Award: LPA Office Renovation

2005

U.S. Green Building Council
LEED®– CI Certified: LPA Irvine Office
Headquarters

**American Institute of Architects
California Council/"Savings by Design"**
Merit Award: Cesar Chavez Elementary School

**Pacific Coast Builders Conference
Gold Nugget Awards**
Best Sustainable Non-Residential Project
Woodland Police Facility

2004

U.S. Green Building Council
LEED® Certified: Woodland Police Facility
LEED® Certified: Cotati Police Facility

**Pacific Coast Builders Conference
Gold Nugget Awards**
Best Sustainable/Green Non-Residential Project
of the Year: Toyota South Campus

2003

U.S. Green Building Council
LEED® Gold: Toyota South Campus

**Governor's Environmental & Economic
Leadership Award/California Environmental
Protection Agency**
Toyota South Campus

**Sustainable Design Leadership Award
CORENET Global**
Toyota South Campus

**American Institute of Architects
California Council/"Savings by Design"**
Merit Award: Premier Automotive Group, North
American Headquarters

**American Institute of Architects
Long Beach/South Bay Chapter**
Honor Award Green Architecture: Toyota South
Campus

2001

U.S. Green Building Council
LEED® Certified: Premier Automotive Group,
North American Headquarters

1992

**Southern California Edison
Design for Excellence**
Certificate of Merit: Irvine Ranch Water District

2005

Orange Public Library
Orange, California

Wal-Mart Experimental Stores
McKinney, Texas and Aurora, Colorado

Mission Motor Sports
Irvine, California

Moreno Valley Sports and Community Center
Moreno Valley, California

Fiesta De Vida Master Planned Community
Indio, California

Eskaton Village Roseville, Master Planned Senior Community
Roseville, California

Santiago Canyon College Student Services Building
Orange, California

Las Positas College, Master Plan
Las Positas, California

Marc Antonio Firebaugh High School
Lynwood Unified School District
Lynwood, California

2004

Rancho Santa Margarita City Hall and Regional Community Center
Rancho Santa Margarita, California

Merage Jewish Community Center of Orange County
Irvine, California

LPA, Inc. "Sustainable Design Lab"
Irvine, California

Woodland Police Station
Woodland, California

Saddleback College, Health Sciences and District Office Building
Mission Viejo, California

Sonoma State University, Student Recreation Center
Rohnert Park, California

Legado Master Planned Community
Dayton Valley, Nevada

E*Trade Financial
Irvine, California

Cesar Chavez Elementary School
Long Beach Unified School District
Long Beach, California

Desert Hot Springs High School Expansion
Palm Springs Unified School District
Desert Hot Springs, California

Laguna Beach High School Modernization
Laguna Beach Unified School District
Laguna Beach, California

Melrose Elementary School
Placentia–Yorba Linda Unified School District
Placentia, California

Witter Ranch Elementary School
Natomas Unified School District
Sacramento, California

Leona Jackson K–8 School
Paramount Park Unified School District
Paramount, California

Woodcrest Elementary School
Riverside Unified School District
Riverside, California

2003

Toyota South Campus
Torrance, California

Southwestern College, Learning Resource Center
Chula Vista, California

Almond Elementary School
Fontana Unified School District
Fontana, California

Norwood Middle School
Grant Joint Union High School District
Sacramento, California

Serra Catholic School Campus Master Plan
Rancho Santa Margarita, California

2002

Mission Viejo City Hall and Library Expansion
Mission Viejo, California

Santa College and Santiago Canyon College, Master Plans
Santa Ana, California

Skyworks Solutions
Irvine, California

Tarbut V'Torah Middle/High School
Irvine, California

2001

Premier Automotive Group, North American Headquarters
Irvine, California

Verizon Wireless
Irvine, California

Sierra Lakes Elementary School
Fontana Unified School District
Fontana, California

2000

Ross/Park Elementary School
Anaheim, California

Sage Hill School
Newport Coast, California

San Diego Jewish Academy
Del Mar, California

1999

California State University Chancellor's Office
Long Beach, California

Mission Imports
Laguna Niguel, California

Moreno Valley Public Safety Facility
Moreno Valley, California

Santiago Canyon College Learning Resource Center
Orange, California

Running Springs Elementary School
Anaheim, California

Ann Soldo Elementary School
Watsonville, California

1998

Anaheim Community Center
Anaheim, California

Paramount Park K–8 Elementary School
Paramount, California

San Juan Capistrano Community Center
San Juan Capistrano, California

Southern California College of Optometry
Fullerton, California

University Montessori
Irvine, California

Toyota Master Plan
Torrance, California

1997

Gemological Institute of America (GIA)
Carlsbad, California

The Chapel at Lake Hills Community Church
Laguna Hills, California

Mission Viejo Library
Mission Viejo, California

Mossimo Corporate Headquarters
Irvine, California

Tarbut V'Torah Community Day School
Irvine, California

University Research Park
Irvine, California

1996

Brea Community Center
Brea, California

Irvine Spectrum Pavilion
Irvine, California

Mission Viejo Town Center
Mission Viejo, California

Playmates Toys, Inc.
Costa Mesa, California

Rancho Bernardo Branch Library
San Diego, California

1995

Amtrak Commuter Station
Van Nuys, California

Anaheim Plaza
Anaheim, California

Chula Vista Library
Chula Vista, California

DWP Telecommunications Headquarters
Van Nuys, California

Faith Community Church
West Covina, California

Garden Grove City Hall
Garden Grove, California

Moreno Valley City Hall
Moreno Valley, California

**Saddleback Valley Community Church
Interim Sanctuary**
Foothill Ranch, California

1994

San Marcos Town Center: City Hall
San Marcos, California

**San Marcos Town Center: Community
Center**
San Marcos, California

San Marcos Town Center: Library
San Marcos, California

Temecula Community Recreation Center
Temecula, California

1993

ASK Computer Corporate Headquarters
Mountain View, California

Bumble Bee Corporate Headquarters
San Diego, California

Continental Retail
El Segundo, California

**California State University
School of Business and Information
Sciences**
San Bernardino, California

Kubota Tractor Corporation
Torrance, California

San Bernardino County Law Library
San Bernardino, California

San Diego Gas and Electric
San Diego, California

Desert Vineyard Christian Fellowship
Lancaster, California

New Venture Christian Fellowship
Oceanside, California

1992

Burbank Gateway Center
Burbank, California

Irvine Ranch Water District
Irvine, California

North Island Federal Credit Union
Chula Vista, California

One Parkside
San Bernardino, California

Palomar College Wellness/Fitness Center
San Marcos, California

1991

Disneyland Hotel
Anaheim, California

El Camino Community Center
Orange, California

Natomas Corporate Center
Sacramento, California

One Venture
Irvine, California

1990

AST Research Corporate Headquarters
Irvine, California

Tustin Marketplace
Tustin, California

Vons Corporate Headquarters
Arcadia, California

1988

Calmat Corporate Headquarters
Los Angeles, California

E.R. Squibb & Sons
Irvine, California

River Center
Tuscon, Arizona

Tuscon Gateway
Tuscon, Arizona

DWP Sun Valley Distribution Headquarters
Sun Valley, Arizona

1987
Pod, Inc.
Santa Ana, California

1986
Tri-City Landing
San Bernardino, California

1985
Hutton Center
Santa Ana, California

State Compensation Insurance Fund
Sacramento, California

1984
Automatic Data Processing (ADP)
La Palma, California

California Center
Sacramento, California

1981
Greystone Phase I
Las Vegas, Nevada

1979
Clubhouse V
Laguna Hills, California

1978
Chapman College Harold Hutton Sports Center
Orange, California

Larkspur Landing
Larkspur, California

STUDIO

Principals

Robert Kupper
Dan Heinfeld
David Gilmore
James Kelly
James Wirick
Christopher Torrey
Steven Kendrick
Glenn Carels
Wendy Rogers
Jon Mills
Richard D'Amato
Joseph Yee
Charles Pruitt
James Kisel
Karen Thomas
Kevin Sullivan

Michael Henning
Gloria Broming
James Raver
Paul Breckenridge
Lawrence Chiu
Don Pender
David Eaves
Richard Musto

Associates

Brandon De Arakal
Chris Lentz
Young Min
Kenneth Murai
Patrick McClintock
Stephen Tiner
Carrick Boshart
Steven Flanagan
Laura Nelson
Keith Hempel
Arash Izadi
Winston Bao
John Robison
Damon Dusterhoft

Staff

Lynette Stabile
Lorrie Ellis
David Duff
Jamie Heidebrink
Kimberly Izadi
Robert Demmond
Deann Collins
Tracy Ettinger
Lisa Luttrell
Gillian Crane
Jeremy Hart
Laura Goforth
Rebecca Snellen van Vollenhoven
Richard Bienvenu
Wendy Robison
Casey Kysoth
Anna New
Tonya Howell
Krista Smallwood
Nick Arambarri
Denise Mendelssohn
Jomay Laio

Kenneth Taylor
Adam De Leon
Justin Kerfoot
Silke Metzler
Michael Rich
Carlyle Aguilar
Mario Hernandez
David Diep
Craig Whitridge
Marc Pange
Kenneth Francis
Lili Ludwig
Kathy Trinh
Nicole Mehta
Jenny Ye
Craig Shulman
Wendy Crenshaw
Rene Pandaeus
Adrienne Tabo
Robin Bugbee
Lindsay Hayward
Karen Folsom
Michael McAllister
Ti Thang
Dylan Blew
Carrie Carbajal
Mamerto Tabora
Wayne van Heel
Michael Endres
Tim McCormack
Franco Brown
Noah Toomey

Asawari Dandekar
Sylvia Situ
Kellie Moore
Paula Wallick
Patricia Rios
Alvaro Lopez
Rolan Castaneda
Cynthia Nei
Myron Veazey
Ozzie Tapia
Alice Kim
Heather Ogg
Sondra Graver
Rita Shiiba
Linda Webb
Claudia Gomez
Arturo Lavenant Jr
Peter Vargas
Jason Willis
Kenneth Lee
Jamey Dobbs
Yvette Sheehan
Dylan Thomas
Lee Schwieterman
Eddie Berumen
Jeremy Fong
Roger Van
Jitendra Kashyap
Kimberly Hoffmaster
Daniel Chong
Samuel Sabin
Victor Giudici

Bill Spence
Elizabeth Hatch
Stephen McMurchie
Edgar Villa
Karen Hildreth
Anthony Arata
Stephen Thorlin
Andrea Blasko
Krislyn Flackus
Kenzie Riesselman
Tommy Ngo
Emiliano Melgazo
Stephen Newsom
Shan Lin
Charles Williams
Carrie Littlejohn
Mark Campos
Chad Puraty
Samuel Lim
Quan Souresrafil
Jana Itzen
Marianella Castillo
Rita Frink
Elaine Johnson
Jefferson Choi
Douglas Cruse
Cristofor Balestreri
Mark Bradbury
Ana Lilia Mendoza
Bernadette Reyes
Carrie Zahradnik
Renilio Cruz

Michael Kaesler
Josh Divelbiss
Bryce Osborn
Brian Boyd
Heidi Roseler
Schiller Cassell III
Afshan Afshar
Katherine Mraw
Mina Roades
Andrea Daliri
Fernando Calderon
James Cleveland
John Gilmore
Stephanie Matsuda
Rogelio Manzo
Hye-Jin Lim
R. Travis Rice
Cynthia Booth
Marc Beique
Gretchen Zeagler
William Itzen
Kenneth Ong
Jin Seo
Angela Chiang
Travis Frye
Mark Wilkerson
Molly Garner
Chad Edgley
Jared Bohonus
Pin Li
Wan-Lian Chang
Maria Calderon-Kurtz
Teresa McLean

Jeffrey Fiftal
Jay Hoskinson
Jessica Miller
Kathy Kia
Tamara Miller
Trent Noll
Mike Janus
Glenn Kubota
Eric Ma
Marc LeGendre
Tiffany Theriot
Iris Tsai
Michelle Russell
Lisa Webb
Adina Delgado
Alice Lee
Andrea Larsen
Callie Gaillard
Marina Bottoni
Nathan Pollet
Rafael Alvarez
Serena Stephenson
Shelly Jones
Danielle Sedory
Luke Kinne
Ben Bravo
Yuko Konishi
Tadashi Yamaguchi
Hormoz Ziaebrahimi
Kevin McCall
Amy Harrington
Laurie Crutchfield
Melody Jiang

PHOTOGRAPHY CREDITS

Front jacket image
Adrian Velicescu

Back jacket image
Cristian D. Costea

Pages: 6, 7, 39-top, 58, 103, 105, 106-right, 108-top
Kellie Moore

Pages: 14, 15, 19, 25, 37, 38, 39-bottom, 40-right, 42, 43, 44, 45, 46, 47, 59, 60, 61, 62, 63, 93-bottom
Adrian Velicescu

Page: 33
Timothy Hursley

Page: 17
Lawrence W. Cheek

Page: 28-bottom
Al Forester

Pages: 26, 27, top 28, 30, 40-left, 41, 50, 58-left, 67-right, 68, 80, 83-top left, 91, 93-top right
LPA

Page: 48
Toyota Motor Sales

Pages: 18, 20, 22, 23, 29, 49, 51, 52, 53, 54, 56, 57, 65, 66, 70, 71, 72, 73, 74, 75, 77, 78, 79, 80, 81, 82, 83, 84, 85, 87, 88, 89, 90, 92, 93-top left, 94, 95, 96, 97, 98, 101, 102, 104, 106, 107-right, 109
Cristian D. Costea